PAST TIME

PAST TIME

*Simulation Football Leagues,
Living in the Past, and Learning
to Love Football Again*

Ted Kluck

LYONS PRESS
Guilford, Connecticut

An imprint of Rowman & Littlefield
Distributed by NATIONAL BOOK NETWORK

Copyright © 2015 by Ted Kluck

British Library Cataloguing in Publication Information Available

Library of Congress Cataloging-in-Publication Data

Kluck, Ted.
Past time : simulation football leagues, living in the past, and learning to love football again / Ted Kluck.
pages cm.
"Distributed by NATIONAL BOOK NETWORK"--T.p. verso.
Includes index.
ISBN 978-1-4930-1696-9 (paper : alk. paper) -- ISBN 978-1-4930-1751-5 (electronic)
1. Football--United States. 2. Football teams--United States. 3. National Football League. 4. Fantasy football (Game) I. Title.
GV954.K49 2015
796.332--dc23

                          2015018822

∞ ™ The paper used in this publication meets the minimum requirements of American National Standard for Information Sciences Permanence of Paper for Printed Library Materials, ANSI/NISO Z39.48-1992.

Printed in the United States of America

For all of the old men

CONTENTS

INTRODUCTION

Don't Look Back

My wife walks into our living room to find me deep in thought, brow furrowed, and scribbling furiously onto a notebook. There are, let's be honest, few benefits to being married to a writer, as we tend to be narcissistic, financially unstable, and given to long, bloviating asides having to do with whatever it is we're doing, which is, of course, the most interesting thing in the world.

One of the benefits, though, is the sublime moment where I run across a beautiful line that I've read (common) or even written (way less common) and then read it to my wife. It's the romantic writerly moment we both dreamed of. And when she walks in to find me deep in thought and deep in notebook, she assumes that I'm crafting something beautiful. She couldn't be more wrong.

"What are you doing?" she asks. Maybe she hopes I'm writing poetry again, which is what I did a lot of early in our marriage, when I was "paid" in copies of literary magazines whose readerships could probably now fit comfortably into our minivan.

"Seriously, what is it?" she says, grabbing the notebook. Her brow furrows when she finds long lists of categorized names—some circled, some with multiple stars drawn next to them. It's the kind of "crazy" that would have found itself onto the Russell Crowe character's walls in *A Beautiful Mind*. Except way less brilliant.

"Derrell Gofourth . . . Kevin Long . . . Bobby Douglass . . . Tim Wilson . . . Larry Csonka . . . Bill Brundige. What is this?"

"It's a list of names," I reply. "It's for my 1977 simulation league roster."

I have found, online, a community of computer nerds and football enthusiasts so deeply rooted in the past and so wholly uninterested in the future that they have created a complicated set of algorithms and computer software that can accurately simulate football games, seasons, and careers using fields of data that already exist on the thousands of players who have, at one time, suited up in the National Football League. All of these players are now old. Some of them are now dead. But they are now the object of my fascination.

"Who does this?" she asks.

"A bunch of old guys—and me."

"How do you know they're old?"

"I'm inferring a lot but, mainly, their names. Names like Ed, Vince, Abe, Ralph, Bill, and George. And how gentleman-ly they are."

"Gentlemanly?"

I'm thirty-seven. I am part of Generation X, and we feel as though we invented snark and cleverness. We also feel like we invented sports-related cleverness and are, for the most part, responsible for the sneering, ironic talking heads that populate ESPN and its offspring. We are a generation of Bill Simmons knockoffs. We're in too many fantasy leagues. We're too cool for everything. We've heard every idea before. We already know what you're about to tell us. We are mostly insufferable.

Irony, when used correctly, can be a weapon of the weak against the strong, but I feel like we live in a world where we all use it all the time for everything regardless of our level of strength or weakness. Being too clever for everything means that I never have to fully commit to anything on an emotional level, which means I'll never get hurt. If I preemptively make fun of my favorite NFL player or my favorite band, movie, or even genre, I'll never be disappointed when that thing (inevitably) disappoints me. I will have been too clever for it.

I don't know when I stopped caring about modern football. I realized it, though, when my son (age eleven) asked me who played in last year's Super Bowl and I couldn't remember, although I can still remember the name and position of every starter on the 1985 Chicago Bears. Regarding modern football and its "wide open" offenses, Nike-inspired Spandex sausage-casing sleeveless jerseys, twenty-four-hour NFL Network coverage, up-to-the-minute fantasy updates, and space age helmets, I just don't care. I watch, occasionally, because it's there, but I'd much rather watch something old.

"Yeah, gentlemanly. I guess what I mean is that they punctuate their e-mails correctly and they're not always trying to be funny."

"That is appealing," she replies.

The online Odyssey Football League began in 2006, with the 1966 NFL season, and has been gradually working its way through NFL history ever since, with franchises "drafting" players before each season per that year's rookie draft. "Coaches" then meet up virtually, crafting game plans, calling plays, changing plays at the virtual line of scrimmage, keeping score, winning, and losing. Players are deployed in ways both similar to and different from the ways they were deployed in real life. Theories are tested. I have theories.

What if NFL teams went back to power offenses like the late 1980s Parcellsian Giants? Would they turn the ball over less? Are running backs over 220 pounds more effective and less likely to get hurt? What if teams went for it on fourth down more often? Can a running quarterback survive if he's deployed more like a running back? How important is a dominant blocking fullback?

And why are there whole groups of people out there this obsessed with the past and (ostensibly) this turned off by the present? Was there something sublimely simple and innocent about the 1970s and 1980s that we're missing today? Was there something in the straightforward presentation of these games that actually enhanced our enjoyment? Were we allowed to dream?

Past Time explores these questions and many others as the author—a jaded journalist, a lifelong football player, and a burned-out coach—spends a year immersed in the late 1970s in hopes of rekindling his love for the game. Part memoir and part Bill Jamesian exploration into "deep" football nerdery, *Past Time* will be both an homage to football's past and a meditation on its present and future.

I

A MEDITATION ON FAILURE

The 1977 Tampa Bay Buccaneers

The first thing I notice is the shoes—the Pony nubbed turf shoes that no doubt kept many orthopedic surgeons in business throughout the better part of the 1970s, 1980s, and 1990s. The idea was that the little rubbery nubs would grab into the short pile of the indoor/outdoor carpet that was first patented in 1965 and originally sold under the ghastly name "Chem-Grass." It was later rebranded as "AstroTurf," which is kind of Jetsonian but way better than ChemGrass.

The shoes strike me as the one thing that has been made *truly* obsolete by modern-day football, which has (thankfully) moved on from the old iteration of AstroTurf and into an era that has reembraced both actual grass and a variety of grass-like synthetic surfaces on which players wear regular cleated shoes. The turf shoes haven't been produced (in nubbed form) since the 1980s, when most players began to realize that basketball shoes were grabby enough on the carpeted surface and that anything else is too grabby. Naturally, I begin a search for my own pair of size-11.5 turf nubs.

The pair I finally find on eBay after a shoe-grail-like search appears to have been sitting in the previous owner's outbuilding since the Bert Jones era, based on their yellowed patina, which is not unlike that of an old newspaper. They are Pony brand, and though the leather is stiff, it breaks in nicely after a couple of wearings, resulting in a super-comfortable and ridiculous-looking pair of shoes that I wear around the house with pride as my wife predictably shakes her head in what I hope is a posture of mockery mixed with love.

Also ridiculous is a tape of the 1977 Tampa Bay Buccaneers that I've acquired, fascinated as I am with the arc of what might have been the worst professional football team in history. The John McKay–led Bucs were awarded a franchise in 1976 and started their history by going 0–14 in spectacularly bad fashion.

The team's woes actually began before they ever set foot on the field, as one of their early expansion draft acquisitions, former Miami Dolphin Doug Swift, had retired from football the day before the draft to enter medical school. They signed a player (running back Anthony Davis) who was still under contract with the Canadian Football League and defensive lineman Pat Toomay, who was believed to have been black-balled due to the publication of his tell-all memoir *The Crunch*.

The tape—from Week Three in 1977—shows two teams very much at opposite ends of the spectrum. The Bucs were losers of sixteen straight and wouldn't win as a franchise until Week Thirteen of the 1977 season. They were led by names like Gary Huff, Anthony Davis, and John McKay—a wide receiver who also happened to be the coach's son. Across the field, the Dallas Cowboys, by contrast, seem to sparkle. Theirs is a star-laden roster, with each name more impressive than the next, boasting players like Thomas "Hollywood" Henderson, Drew Pearson, Tony Dorsett, and Roger Staubach. The game takes place on a perfect fall day (seventy-four degrees and sunny) on a technicolor-radiant plastic surface in a then-perfect stadium. The Bucs seem horribly out of place.

The Bucs roster is similar to mine in that there are precious few building blocks, surrounded by a pervasive dearth of talent. Tampa drafted two Selmon brothers—Lee Roy, who would become a Hall of Famer, and his also-good brother Dewey—both of whom would become cornerstones of the defense. They got Dave Pear in the expansion draft, who would play in a Pro Bowl. Cornerback Mark Cotney and linebacker Richard Wood will go on to play with distinction. But those players are surrounded by a cast of veteran also-rans led by quarterback Gary Huff. My sim team's future left tackle, Charley Hannah, is a starter at *defensive* end for this Buc squad.

This game marks the first time that Anthony Davis and Ricky Bell have lined up together in the same backfield—noteworthy because both are former USC Trojan stars but really for no other reason. It is a bad Tampa team trying to grasp at straws and create matchups, which is something with which I was well acquainted during my own 1977 season.

The Cowboys of the late 1970s were the league's model example of team building through the draft. Their defensive line boasted superstars in Randy White, Harvey Martin, and

Ed "Too Tall" Jones, not to mention a holdover from a bygone era in Jethro Pugh, who is perhaps best known for getting blocked by Green Bay Packer Jerry Kramer to lose the Ice Bowl on Bart Starr's quarterback sneak. Their defensive back end features Charlie Waters and Cliff Harris. To say that they are loaded would be an understatement. That would be like a current NFL defense that featured Mario Williams, Julius Peppers, Ndamukong Suh, Troy Polamalu, and Adrian Wilson—all in their primes.

Watching this game is really like watching a good NFL team play a mid-level USFL team. What few bright spots Tampa has are overshadowed or negated by the fact that they can't block anyone consistently. If they manage to block Randy White on a given play, Pugh and Martin are in the backfield to make the play. The Bucs were outscored 412–125 in 1976 and finished dead last in yardage and points scored. By contrast, the winless Detroit Lions of 2008 were outscored 517–268, which seems almost respectable by comparison.

This all serves to put my 1977 "expansion" sim season into sharper perspective. I won two games and lost twelve but was never really blown out and managed to stay "in" most games despite bad quarterbacking from Richard Todd (whom I later traded) and Brian Sipe, who would take a few years to develop. I stayed in the games by running the ball a lot, grinding out some first downs, and managing to cobble together a decent defense with smoke and mirrors. Still, like the 1976 and 1977 Bucs, I'll need to somehow create a real infusion of talent in order to be even remotely competitive in the 1978 season.

Dallas, playing at home, is in their customary white jersey with the Cowboy silver/blue pants and iconic helmet. Tampa is in their (my opinion) sublime orange-creamsicle uniform, which sparkles in sharp contrast to the Arena Football League–worthy pewter/red/black version they wore in 2014. Given the fact that Tampa's offense was so bad, their defense is on the field for much of the game, giving me an opportunity to appreciate how good some of their defensive players actually are. Lee Roy Selmon had unique, Lawrence Taylor–like skills.

Various oddities:

1. Dallas's backup quarterback, Danny White, is also its starting punter—something you'd never see in today's NFL given the astronomical quarterback salaries and the league's China doll approach to quarterback safety. My son Tristan: "Half the quarterbacks in the NFL today, if you look at them wrong, they throw a flag."

2. There is a Miller Lite commercial starring Paul Hornung, Dick Butkus, Ben Davidson, Bubba Smith, and Rodney Dangerfield all hanging out in a retro bar and cracking wise. Me, to my wife: "That makes me want to drink beer." It's an advertising aesthetic (put a bunch of exceedingly cool people into a room, un-ironically) that we don't see anymore, in part because today's athletes and even ex-athletes are savvier and, I guess, more paranoid about being beer pitchmen. But also they're decidedly less cool and charismatic than the Butkus/Hornung/Davidson/Namath/Bert Jones crowd. Who would advertisers show hanging out in a bar from today's NFL? Who would fans actually want to hang out with?

3. Random things that CBS was promoting via its "CBS Sports Spectacular" included world middleweight full-contact karate and the World's Strongest Man Competi-

tion, featuring the "steel bar bend" contest, in which, according to the clip, contestants bend a steel bar over their heads. I miss the 1970s.

4. An ad exclaims, "Tomorrow night is Elvis night!" complete with video of a jumpsuit-era Elvis, causing my son to point out that "Elvis looks a lot different there than in most pictures I've seen of him." Again, I miss the 1970s. "I love watching these old games," Tristan adds. "I like how everything wasn't all technical. They don't always tell you the score on-screen. You have to actually watch the game. I kind of even like the commercials."

5. "They don't throw as many flags," Tristan observes. "In a regular game right now, there'd be like eight penalties already." He's right. Officiating, in the modern game, has taken on a more central role with our obsession with replay, coaches' challenges, and Mike Pereira's in-game NFL-approved public relations spin of the officiating, creating an atmosphere in which endless dialogue about officiating has dominated almost every game narrative.

6. A vignette in which the network talking heads explained that Tampa running back Anthony Davis "hit his head on the hotel room sink the night before the Minnesota game and played dizzy the entire afternoon," the implication clearly being that Davis was probably so hammered that night that the world-class athlete couldn't make it from the bed to the toilet without somehow running his head into the sink on the way.

7. Disgraced baseball legend Pete Rose shills for the "Zenith Color Sentry" television, which was the kind that came in a gigantic wooden console that sat on the floor of your living room.

8. There is an ad for a television drama called *Young Dan'l Boone*: "A settler's betrayal turns the Indians against Dan'l Boone!" (politically incorrect story lines you'd never see today).

As I watch all of this Bucs futility, a few lessons are emerging for me:

1. Having an elite pass rusher doesn't make that much of a difference when surrounded by a team that is otherwise uniformly crappy. As remarkable as Selmon was (and he put a beating on Dallas tackle Ralph Neely in this game), he couldn't overcome an offense that couldn't get a first down and keep him off the field for any amount of time, and was eventually worn down. Also excellent is Tampa linebacker Richard Wood, though he is a victim of the same phenomenon as Selmon. Wood notches a fumble return for a touchdown in the second quarter on Tony Dorsett's first carry.

2. That said, Tampa's offense had a dynamic skill player or two (Ricky Bell comes to mind here) but was undone by its thoroughly unremarkable offensive line. Tampa's starting interior line included the following players, with notes on how they were acquired:

   Left tackle Dave Reavis / Pittsburgh Steelers / 5th round / 106th pick / 1973
   Left guard Jeff Winans / Buffalo Bills / 2nd round / 32nd pick / 1973
   Center Dan Ryczek / Washington Redskins / 13th round / 322nd pick / 1971

Right guard Dan Medlin / Oakland Raiders / 6th
round / 131st pick / 1972
Right tackle Darryl Carlton / Miami Dolphins / 1st
round / 23rd pick / 1975

3. Carlton is the only first-round pick in the bunch, and he
was a disappointment. The other linemen are equally
underwhelming. I'll need to build my expansion team by
prioritizing my offensive front. I used a 1977 draft pick
to acquire Hannah, who won't play offensive tackle until
1979 but will then play it very well for almost a decade.
I'll also have solid starters in center Carl Mauck and
guard Randy Rasmussen. I'll place a high priority on
getting a starting tackle out of the 1978 draft.

4. Tampa didn't have any receivers who could create
matchup problems for their opponents. Their starting
wideouts were former fifth-round pick Morris Owens
and the coach's son John McKay, who was a former
sixteenth-round pick of the Cleveland Browns. Their
most effective pass play seemed to be "have Huff scram-
ble for his life and hope that the coverage breaks down."
Owens, their leading receiver, had only thirty-four
catches. I traded for wide receiver Reggie Rucker, a
high- to mid-grade starter and playmaker, who gave me
one decent option in 1977. However, without another
pass-game option, I was extremely limited, as teams
would load up coverage on Rucker. This is a truism even
in today's NFL, as offenses devoid of receiving talent
(like the Jaguars and Jets) can't create matchups and
struggle to score points. On the other side of the field,
Dallas had Drew Pearson, Golden Richards, and Butch
Johnson at receiver, along with two better-than-average

tight ends in Billy Joe Dupree and Jay Saldi. There was no conceivable way for Tampa to cover all of them. I'd like to acquire a good tight end if for no other reason that I could ease some of the coverage on Rucker.

5. Bucs quarterback Gary Huff is really bad. Whether this is primarily a function of his bad line and his mediocre receivers or he's actually that bad is unclear. Either way, I'll need to do something about the quarterback position until Sipe starts playing better in the late 1970s and early 1980s (at which point he actually gets quite good).

6. Dallas running back Tony Dorsett is a really good ballcarrier. But how good would he be behind Tampa's offensive line? I was pleasantly surprised at how well my ordinary backs (e.g., Dexter Bussey) performed for me in 1977. Bussey was on pace to gain over 1,000 yards in only fourteen games were it not for a season cut short by injuries. This has me thinking that I should make big investments in other positions and could count on Bussey types to keep getting me around four yards per carry. I don't need to break the bank for a Dorsett type in order to have a good run game. Out of loyalty to my childhood hero Walter Payton, it's worth mentioning that (unlike Payton) Dorsett had absolutely no interest in blocking.

7. Dorsett is good, in part, because of the lead blocking of the underrated Robert Newhouse. I want to make it a point to always have an effective lead blocker on my roster so that I can test out my run-centric I-formation theories.

This game has the mood and vibe of a scrimmage in terms of intensity. The Cowboys seem bored, and Tampa looks demoralized. Even Dallas's fans seem thoroughly listless and uninterested in spite of their team's success. Texas Stadium is nearly silent. By Week Three of the 1977 season, the Tampa offense still hadn't scored a touchdown. That cold streak continued against Dallas. Huff finished the game a dreadful eight for twenty-three with 107 yards and two picks. Backfield star Ricky Bell was held to seven yards on three carries. For a game that in NFL historical terms was infinitely forgettable, I enjoyed it a ton and learned a lot. Watching a bad team with a few good players has given me a clearer picture of what I want to do with the few resources I do have—namely, a handful of players with a future (Rucker, Sipe, Bussey, Rasmussen, Mauck, and linebacker Mark Arneson) and a full allotment of 1978 picks.

2

RUNNING ON EMPTY

The Myth of the Franchise Quarterback

I meet every few weeks with a real estate developer/film producer on a turf field in East Lansing, Michigan, where he throws me the entire route tree, and I chug along in my turf shoes and receiver's gloves, catching slants, outs, posts, post-corners, and fades. We are both in our late thirties and have absolutely no good reason to be doing this save for an abiding love of football. He was a small-college quarterback in the 1990s and has never kicked the habit.

"Don't pull a hamstring," giggles a Michigan State women's lacrosse player as I haul in a sweet fade over my shoulder in the fading sunlight. It would have been a perfect moment—the sun, the turf, the girl, and the MSU band practicing in the background—except that I'm pretty sure she was making fun of us.

The exercise of throwing with Nathaniel each week notwithstanding, it does raise an interesting question: If a late thirties, ex–small-college quarterback can throw the entire tree pretty accurately, why is it so hard to play quarterback in the NFL, and why is it so hard to *draft* quarterbacks in the NFL?

My ESPN.com draft study, which looked at a fifteen-year chunk of NFL first-round picks from 1989 through 2003, analyzed the success or failure of each player selected in that time frame, ultimately determining a bust percentage for each position. As such, I had to determine a simple "success metric" so that I could apply it to each player. For quarterbacks, my "bust bar" was set at eighty or more games played in the league, plus a positive touchdown-to-interception ratio. A Pro Bowl appearance or a Super Bowl win (e.g., Trent Dilfer, "the ultimate game manager") would allow for overlooking transgressions in other areas.

What the study revealed is that quarterbacks "busted"—or failed to meet the above criteria—53 percent of the time, making it the riskiest position on the field to draft in the first round. I'll revisit the study below, with updated draft classes, but first I want to discuss the ethereal label of franchise quarterback. How important is it to have a franchise quarterback, and what does that even mean?

THE FRANCHISE QUARTERBACK: PERCEPTION AND REALITY

When teams draft a quarterback within the first twenty picks of the first round of the draft, they do so with the intention of making that player their franchise quarterback—meaning that he needs to not only play the position well but also, ostensibly, help sell tickets, jerseys, and other merchandise while becoming the public face of the franchise. This is even more imperative, it seems, with quarterbacks drafted in the top ten.

Teams do this in hopes of landing the next John Elway or Troy Aikman—guys who "look the part" and can sell the image of the position as well as provide elite production on the field. In the cases of Elway and Aikman, both landed in what turned out to be ideal circumstances. Elway famously gamed the 1983 draft by refusing to play for Frank Kush in Baltimore (undoubtedly a wise move) and found his way to Denver, where he inherited a not-bad Bronco team that had some holdover offensive weapons, including Rick Upchurch and Steve Watson, and a bunch of guys on defense, such as Dennis Smith, Karl Mecklenburg, and Tom Jackson, who would be with the Broncos through their early Super Bowl years. In his rookie season, the Broncos went 9–7 and made the playoffs.

Aikman's franchise quarterback experience was a little different. He went to a Dallas Cowboy team with a new coach (Jimmy Johnson) for the first time in the history of the franchise and seemingly very little else. However, Johnson was already beginning to put the pieces in place, as joining Aikman on the roster were players like fullback Daryl Johnston, center Mark Stepnoski, and wide receiver Michael Irvin—all of whom would be mainstays throughout the Cowboy dynasty. Perhaps Aikman's most important teammate was running back Herschel Walker, whose trade would enable Johnson to draft many of the cornerstones of the franchise.

The point of both of these illustrations is that even though both players were first-overall picks in their respective drafts, they found themselves in situations that weren't as bad as they may have seemed. That said, a lot of high picks are used on quarterbacks who are immediately grafted into hopeless situations and fail to thrive. These teams are trying to re-create an Elway–Aikman–Marino dynamic in situations that are geared toward their young quarterbacks' failure.

Take, for example, Cleveland's Tim Couch, who may have been the product of a gimmicky college offense but who, according to many in the league, had what it took to be a viable NFL quarterback. You'll recall that Couch was drafted first overall by the expansion version of the Browns after the original Browns had moved to Baltimore.

Couch struggled. His best running backs were the unremarkable Terry Kirby (452 yards) and Karim Abdul-Jabbar (350 yards), whose claim to fame was that he shares a name with a famous basketball player. Couch's best receiver was Kevin Johnson (sixty-six catches), whose claim to fame is that he also shares a name with a famous basketball player. Couch took a staggering fifty-six sacks as a rookie and (not surprisingly) had trouble staying healthy throughout a short career that ended in 2003 without so much as a whiff of a playoff appearance. Couch's career was a lot like David Carr's in that regard (as well as others). Carr was the first pick of the expansion Houston Texans, where he came with a face-of-the-franchise "face" and had a similar experience in that he was sacked all the time and didn't have much of anything to speak of around him. In fact, both Carr and Couch were sacked so often that pundits wondered if that (the sacks) "ruined" them mentally for any other quarterbacking experiences that they may have had down the line. There's probably something to that.

There are plenty of quarterbacks who aren't first-overall picks who still come with franchise expectations and fail to deliver on those expectations—guys like Cade McNown, Joey

Harrington, Kyle Boller, Matt Leinart, and Vince Young. McNown had only fifteen career starts in a two-year career. What a strange résumé for a first-round pick. One such guy was supposed to be Elway's heir in Denver—Jay Cutler.

I've been thinking a lot about the career arcs of two petulant quarterbacks (would-be franchises) who had huge arm strength and huge problems getting along with seemingly everyone: Jeff George and Cutler.

Both were first-round draft choices (George was first overall in 1990) from middling college programs (Illinois for George, Vanderbilt for Cutler). Both possessed outrageous arm talent and burgeoning reputations for being surly and truculent with coaches, teammates, and the media. These concerns were initially (and for some years after) overlooked (because of arm talent).

Both players have been given way more chances than they deserve(d) to carry the franchise quarterback mantle. Both players worked their way through a litany of offensive coordinators and head coaches—in Cutler's case, Mike Shanahan, Josh McDaniels, Ron Turner, Mike Martz, and Lovie Smith come to mind. Initially, all these relationships started with statements like "[Name of Coach] is really getting the most out of Jay Cutler! They're really getting along well and are on the same page!" These statements usually lasted half a season (at best) before the relationship soured and one of the men was gone (usually the coach, in whom there was a less significant financial investment than the one made in Cutler or George).

Both men were on their second franchise by age twenty-nine. George was on his third by age thirty-one. Both were given inexplicably huge contracts by teams that still thought they had franchise quarterback potential despite perpetually underperforming in the area of wins and losses.

George was 46–78 in his career starts. Cutler is a slightly better 58–51, which is a function of playing on better teams—such is the difference between being picked in the eleventh spot (Cutler) and the first spot (George).

Both men have almost identical touchdown-to-interception ratios (167/118 for Cutler, 154/113 for George). Completion percentages hover around 60 percent for both (61.4 for Cutler, 57.9 for George).

Neither has much in the way of a playoff résumé. George was 1–2 in playoff starts, while Cutler is 1–1. Both showed that they were capable of explosive statistical output, with Cutler topping 4,500 yards in 2008 (as a Denver Bronco) and George going for over 4,100 yards in his best season—1995 with the Atlanta Falcons.

For me, two questions remain. First, when did we start perceiving Jeff George as a journeyman, and when will we start perceiving Cutler in the same way? Second, is there any hope left for Cutler as a franchise quarterback?

(As an aside, I was about to put former first-overall Carson Palmer into the same category, but Palmer has been better statistically [over 4,000 yards four times and a lifetime 62.6 completion percentage], if not in the playoffs [0–2 lifetime].)

I like Cutler. I think he's tough, and, like everyone else, I think he possesses really special physical attributes. I'd like to see him have success.

I think Cutler's only hope remains in a "twilight of career" scenario involving him playing for less money (humbling) for a coach who won't be intimidated or manipulated by him. There aren't many coaches like that left in pro football. Bill

Belichick and Tom Coughlin come to mind, but both have quarterbacks already with whom they will both probably retire. Pete Carroll seems to be something of a "quarterback whisperer," but he has a young guy, Russell Wilson, who will ostensibly be in the position for a long time. More likely, Cutler's career will go the way of George's. He may wander in the proverbial desert to franchises like Tennessee, Oakland, and Houston that are perpetually quarterback poor. I hope this isn't the case. I hope he finds harmony with Marc Trestman and the talented receivers in Chicago. I hope the Bears remember who they are (i.e., a team with an elite running back and a history of sound defense) and stop being at odds with the idea of running the football.

Each year, as the draft approaches, it seems like the league and the media conspire to "sell" us on a number of franchise-type quarterbacks. Sometimes, as in the case of Andrew Luck, those prospects actually have the résumé to accompany the hype. Sometimes, as in the case of players like E. J. Manuel and (gasp) Blaine Gabbert and (gasp again) Christian Ponder, they are creations of the media and front offices that are over-eager to "excite the fan base" and put a new player in the most important position on the field. Often, those players go to bad teams (like Jacksonville), where they are immediately thrown into the fray (Gabbert started fifteen games as a rookie on an epically bad Jaguars team), immediately bludgeoned, and sometimes ruined for good. The question is, were they ruined by a bad circumstance, or were they bad to begin with?

The Jaguars appear to be serial franchisers, having been down this road with Gabbert, Byron Leftwich (no Pro Bowls), and now 2014 first-rounder Blake Bortles. The most successful quarterback in the history of the franchise has been Mark Brunell, who came to the Jaguars after a year as Brett Favre's understudy in Green Bay. Brunell made three Pro Bowls and took the team to several playoff appearances.

Gabbert is an interesting study. He had only had twenty-seven career starts—all of them with a dreadful, weaponless Jaguars offense. His rookie numbers, based on touchdown-to-interception ratio and completion percentage, were better than a lot of guys who went on to legendary careers. He had more yards, more touchdowns, and fewer interceptions than Troy Aikman as a rookie, yet he is universally accepted as a bust. Vinny Testaverde, by comparison, was statistically miserable for most of his twenties, but Gabbert is already, basically, done. Strange. Perhaps he is viewed as a product of a gimmicky college offense (more on that below).

Gabbert completed 64 percent of his passes in his final year in Missouri's spread offense—a number that may have been artificially inflated due to the number of quick, lateral throws quarterbacks make out of the spread. But at any rate, he was said to have had "ideal" tangibles for the position—he stood 6'4" and had a strong arm with which to make "all the throws," and he had the kind of Golden Boy look that scouts like because, let's face it, scouts are human and are susceptible to that sort of thing. Mike Mayock gushed over Gabbert at his Pro Day workout, explaining that he would be "the first quarterback" taken and pontificating about the quality of his footwork. Gabbert ran a 4.6-second forty-yard dash, making him faster than noted "running" quarterbacks, including Tim Tebow and Cam Newton (who was actually the first quarterback and the first player taken in 2011). Gabbert was the third quarterback taken, behind Cam Newton, on whom the jury is still very much out, and Jake Locker, who appears to have also been a bust. The other first-round quarterback selected in that draft was Ponder, who was dreadful in his starts in Minnesota and has already been permanently replaced by new savior Teddy Bridgewater. The best quarterbacks in that draft were Andy Dalton and Colin Kaepernick, both of whom were second-round selections. Incidentally, as dreadful as that draft was for quarterbacks, it was a sensational defensive end draft, producing J. J. Watt, Aldon Smith, Robert Quinn, Ryan Kerrigan, and Cameron Jordan. My ESPN study showed that defensive end is a much easier position to project and is thus a "safer" first-round investment, and the 2011 draft certainly bears that out.

Gabbert's NFL washout—and, in fact, the broader discussion of inflated college completion percentage numbers— seems to negate a prevailing trend that one can project NFL quarterback success based solely on college completion percentage numbers and college starts. In March 2006, *Football Outsiders* published a piece titled "College Quarterbacks through the Prism of Statistics," which stated, "Based on my research the two most predictive college statistics are completion percentage and games started."[1] The piece goes on to explain that the "games started" metric is important because it gives scouts adequate film with which to assess which quarterbacks are legitimate prospects and which are just products of a college system. Completion percentage is self-explanatory, the idea being that if a quarterback can't complete a high percentage of passes in college, then he won't magically start doing so at the professional level. It then predicted that Matt Leinart, Vince Young, and Jay Cutler would all be NFL stars based on the metric. Leinart and Young are now out of football, and

Cutler may be on his way to being released by the Chicago Bears and has been, largely, a disappointment. Oops. Gabbert was a two-year starter at Missouri and had the previously mentioned impressive completion percentage because of his spread offense. As such, he "should" have had a more successful run as an NFL starter. This proves, in part, that money-ball types of principles are harder to apply to an NFL context. The numbers just don't work out as nicely because there are so many other variables and moving parts.

Even the "experts" can't get their stories straight regarding Gabbert. Upon his trade to the San Francisco 49ers before the 2014 season, analyst Steve Mariucci said, "He's not going to give you anything with his legs," while another former head coach, Herm Edwards, said, "He's a mobile guy." Which one is it?

Gabbert made his first career start in Week Three of the 2011 season at Carolina against fellow rookie Cam Newton. There was an initial flush of excitement surrounding Newton's early games (he passed for over 400 yards in each of his first two starts) that wasn't there for Gabbert. Essentially, the Panthers did with Newton what the Redskins did with Robert Griffin III early on, which was that they tailored the offense to make it look a lot like the simplified offenses those players ran in college in that there were some zone-read principles in place as well as simple, half-field reads with often only two receivers in play. The 49ers did this early on with Colin Kaepernick, who also enjoyed a great deal of early success but has since plateaued. Kaepernick may be the fastest quarterback in the league in terms of pure foot speed and athleticism, but he struggles to move in the pocket with his eyes downfield and, as of this writing in Week Fourteen of the 2014 season, is leading the league in sacks taken. Meanwhile, two of the least athletic quarterbacks in the league—Tom Brady and Peyton Manning—consistently take very few sacks because of their ability to make subtle adjustments in the pocket with their eyes downfield. This may be yet another indictment of college spread schemes and their inability to get quarterbacks ready for the next level.

This seems, at least for now, to be the career arc of the spread quarterback: a fast start, followed by a pretty deadly plateau in which the player is asked to be more of a "pocket" passer, can't (or won't) do it, and is either benched (Griffin) or settles into mediocrity.

Newton's early tape study shows a trademark ability to keep plays alive by running around as well as a very strong arm. He could whip the ball downfield from a variety of angles, which is a handy skill to have if you're going to be running around a lot. Six of Newton's first eleven plays were out of the shotgun, and there was one designed run for him. He looked extremely comfortable taking his drops and throwing to veteran receivers like Steve Smith, Greg Olsen, and Jeremy Shockey.

By contrast, Gabbert began his first NFL start under center and, after a couple of Maurice Jones-Drew runs were stuffed, went to work in the shotgun on a third-and-long. Jones-Drew was Gabbert's best offensive teammate in 2011, as his starring receivers were Mike Thomas and Jason Hill, both of whom are now out of football. Gabbert's first series ended on a safety, as emerging Carolina pass rusher Greg Hardy exploded around right tackle Guy Whimper and sacked Gabbert in the end zone. It was a harbinger of things to come. His second series—another three-and-out—ended on a sack as well.

His last NFL start, in October 2013, was remarkably similar. He went 9–19 for 181 yards and two picks against a very mediocre St. Louis Rams team. The uniforms were different, the head coach was different (Gus Bradley), but the results were the same. Jones-Drew was still there, and Jacksonville had tried to upgrade its offensive talent, drafting highly touted tackle prospect Luke Joeckel and talented but troubled wideout Justin Blackmon.

His first series, again, ended in a three-and-out and featured a throw to a covered receiver and a sack. None of Gabbert's receivers could get open, and Gabbert didn't seem to know what to do when that happened. He did manage to hit a wide-open Blackmon on a skinny post in the first quarter that Blackmon took to the house. It would be the final bright spot in Gabbert's career to this point. He throws an ugly pick-six late in the first quarter when, under minimal duress in the pocket, he sails a long throw late over the middle that is returned to the house by Rams safety Matt Giordano.

He later fumbled twice on sacks, where each time he showed skittish feet in a collapsing pocket. His last pass as a starter was batted down by Trumaine Johnson, and he was replaced in the third quarter by Chad Henne, who has had as consistent a run as a Jacksonville starting quarterback as anyone in recent years (which isn't saying much).

So what's the solution to the Gabbert problem? Minimizing the position.

MINIMIZING THE POSITION: BELICHICK
WITHOUT BRADY

In 1994—his best season as a coach in a pre–Tom Brady world—Cleveland Browns head coach Bill Belichick went 11–5 with game manager Vinny Testaverde (who, incidentally, had already once washed out as a franchise quarterback). Testaverde was drafted first overall in 1987 out of the University of Miami by a dreadful Tampa Bay Buccaneers franchise that, after a few hopeful years in the late 1970s and early 1980s, was mired in failure. Interestingly, Testaverde took a physical and mental beating in his last collegiate game—an experience some think may have "ruined" him in his transition to the pro level. Vinny threw an epic thirty-five interceptions in 1988, a season in which he started all but one game. In fairness to him, however, it should be noted that his most significant offensive "weapons" were Bruce Hill and Lars Tate.

I found some tape of an early (1991) Testaverde/Bucs game. Even this experience—finding tape—is significant because it's so easy for today's fan to access and break down the same kind of tape that only coaches could previously access and break down. Couple this with social media, and every league fan base has 8.2 million "analysts" screaming for change. It's no wonder that owners can't commit to a quarterback. What's interesting is that by 1991, Testaverde was already several years into a, by then, famously dreadful career. Testaverde failed to throw more touchdowns than interceptions in *each* of his first six seasons in the league. He failed to post a winning record in any of those seasons. It would have been completely logical for the league to have given up on him, except that if they had, they would have missed a lot of productive and even Pro Bowl–caliber seasons.

The creamsicle uniforms of the Bucs are sweet. At the time of the game, they are 2–11, facing a Giants team that is defending its Super Bowl title but is doing so without Bill Parcells. The 1991 Giants are your classic quarterback-minimizing team, continuing the trend they perfected in 1990. This team was still awesome and had the very much still awesome Lawrence Taylor—along with Carl Banks, Pepper Johnson, and Gary Reasons—leading the defense. The 1980s had some hellaciously good linebacking corps (e.g., Mike Singletary, Otis Wilson, and Wilber Marshall). They feature a talented young "big back" (more on that later) and the premier fullback in the game at the time (Maurice Carthon). Being a former fullback, I have a ton of appreciation for a guy like Maurice Carthon. Some may not remember that he helped Herschel Walker set a pro football record for rushing yards in a season when both were members of the New Jersey Generals in the USFL. Incidentally, the game featured another former USFL star in running back Gary Anderson, who was sorely underutilized as a Tampa Bay Buc. Anderson was a dynamic player who, under different circumstances, could have easily ended up being a Roger Craig–type star.

"Here comes Vinny Testaverde . . . who is having a really below-average season," says Verne Lundquist, who pauses, it seems, trying to find something nice to say but failing.

The 1991 Bucs are an interesting team—and by interesting, I mean bad. Their defense featured a washed-up and overweight Dexter Manley, who in his prime in the 1980s was one of the most feared pass rushers and one of the league's most quotable idiots. The rest of the Tampa front seven featured an assortment of high-priced first-round disappointments, including Keith McCants and Broderick Thomas. They are mired in their ninth consecutive losing season. They had given up forty-one sacks coming into the week. Their best player is probably left offensive tackle Paul Gruber, who could have started for almost anyone in the league but who was also rendered almost meaningless because of the lack of talent around him (more on that phenomenon in a later chapter). Testaverde's second-best teammate is tight end Ron Hall, whom he routinely overthrows. Hall wears gigantic shoulder pads, which nobody does anymore. And all of the jerseys have actual fabric on them as opposed to elastic sausage casings that players shoehorn themselves into these days. (I now, officially, sound like my father.)

Testaverde is dreadful on this tape. His footwork is a jangled and nervous mess—he looks terrified in every collapsing pocket that he's in. His throwing motion is long and elaborate, which seems to suggest to the defense, "I'm throwing the ball now, and you have plenty of time to jump the route." A low point comes in the first quarter when a shotgun snap ricochets off his orange facemask. What's interesting is that most of this Testaverde-related ineptitude happened outside the consciousness of most NFL fans. We were vaguely aware that Tampa Bay was terrible and that Testaverde was a disappointment, but it didn't register in the same way it does today, when every one of Blaine Gabbert's throws has been dissected and analyzed by a variety of network talking heads and millions of casual fans. Many of today's quarterbacks are written off before they even get started.

So when and how did things change for Testaverde, who looked so unredeemable in 1991?

His career took an interesting turn for the better after the Belichick experience in Cleveland. He moved with the old Browns to Baltimore, where he enjoyed a Pro Bowl season as a thirty-three-year-old in 1996 and another one as a New York Jet in 1998 at age thirty-five. Testaverde even logged significant starts in 2007 at age forty-four as a Carolina Panther. This begs the question: how important is youth? We tend to think of pro football as a young man's game, but the success of aging quarterbacks (Testaverde, Rich Gannon, etc.) makes me wonder. It should be noted that Testaverde's best season statistically came in 1998 when he was playing for Bill Parcells, who was famous for deemphasizing the quarterback position.

Legendary NFL quarterback Earl Morrall, who played through age forty-one, said the following in George Plimpton's book *Mad Ducks and Bears* about what improves, for a quarterback, with age: "What did improve, and only by a fraction of a second, was the ability to shift from the main receiver and throw the ball almost instantaneously to an alternate. John Unitas had always been the best at that." Unitas played through age forty. Hall of Fame quarterback Steve Young had his *first* Pro Bowl season at age thirty-one and his last at age thirty-seven. He played until age thirty-eight.

In 2002, Jon Gruden won a Super Bowl in Tampa Bay with Brad Johnson starting at quarterback and Shaun King making significant starts in his stead. Johnson was a former ninth-round pick and was thirty-four years old at the time, while King, a second-round selection, never really panned out as an NFL starter. The Johnson-led Bucs won with a great defense led by Warren Sapp, Derrick Brooks, and John Lynch and an adequate running game fueled by Mike Alstott and Michael Pittman.

Gruden went 12–4 in 2000 with the well-traveled Rich Gannon as his starting quarterback. Gannon was thirty-five that season, and the Raiders were his third NFL team.

In the intervening years, Gruden has made a living talking about future franchise quarterbacks on his ESPN special *Gruden's QB Camp*, yet ironically he never had a traditional (via the draft) "franchise" quarterback in his successful tenure as a head coach. Essentially, Gruden is talking about a concept—drafting the first-round quarterback—that he may not even believe in himself. He did, in fact, breathe life into the careers of lots of aging castoff quarterbacks, including, at one time or another, Brian Griese and Jeff Garcia. People forget that even his star early pupil, Brett Favre, was something of a reclamation project in Green Bay, coming via a trade with the Atlanta Falcons, where he was a seldom-used backup.

What's interesting is that although Belichick is considered a defensive guru and Gruden an offensive mastermind, both coaches succeeded at minimizing the quarterback position when they needed to. Brad Johnson completed a high percentage of passes (62.3 percent) to an adequate but far-from-legendary stable of receivers, including an overrated Keyshawn Johnson and an underrated Keenan McCardell, and didn't turn the ball over (twenty-two touchdowns and only six picks). Although it is a pejorative term, Johnson managed the game. Johnson threw a lot of passes to his backs that season, as both Pittman (fifty-nine catches) and Alstott (thirty-five catches) were able receivers out of the backfield.

Perhaps the modern-day king of minimizing the quarterback was Bill Parcells, who ball-controlled his way to two titles in 1986 and 1990 as head coach of the New York Giants. The Giants were twenty-second in the league in pass attempts in 1986 and twenty-seventh in the same category in 1990. Besides Mark Bavaro, a tight end, casual fans would be hard pressed to name a wide receiver from those Giant teams. Those teams protected the football. The 1990 Giants were ranked first in the league in giveaways. They won with a punishing running game, a conservative passing game, and a very good defense led by Lawrence Taylor.

What's interesting is that when he matriculated to New England as a head coach, Parcells seemed to undergo a paradigm shift in offensive philosophy. In 1993, 1994, and 1995, the Patriots ranked fifth, first, and first, respectively, in the league in pass attempts, which is strange given that they were helmed by a young and not-yet-good Drew Bledsoe, who turned the ball over a lot. Perhaps it's because Parcells lacked his usual bell-cow running back, filling the spot with (among others) journeymen, including Leonard Russell, an aging Marion Butts, and Corey Croom.

It's no secret that the NFL of 2014 is a pass-happy league in which rules are getting more offense friendly by the year. However, I still wonder why more teams aren't trying to reimplement the Parcells model? It could be because colleges are no longer producing linemen who can line up in a three-point stance and run block.

3

EVERY WHICH WAY
BUT LOOSE

The Appeal of 1978

The year 1977 was a tough one for my Detroit Lions sim squad, which was basically an expansion team made up of castoffs that wouldn't have stuck on other rosters in the league. The previous owner had traded away all of my 1977 draft choices, and the only player with any "name" value on my roster was quarterback Joe Theismann, whom I didn't care for in real life. I decided to claw my way back into the 1977 draft by trading away some old players for draft choices as well as younger players with upside. I turned aging running back Preston Pearson into a fourth-round choice that I used on Charley Hannah, brother of Hall of Famer John Hannah, who came into the league out of Alabama as a defensive end but who ended up anchoring the Oakland/Los Angeles Raiders offensive line for a decade. He'll eventually replace one of my geriatric tackles.

I then traded my other aging back, Calvin (father of NBA star Grant) Hill, for a young Denver defensive end named Barney Chavous, who played well into the late 1980s and was a consistent sack producer for the Broncos. And with my suspect secondary, I'll need every single sack I can get.

I'll also have to address my one-receiver offense, laden with old linemen and question marks at running back. I want to run the ball—a lot. But I need players to do it. I signed the aging Pete Banaszak to handle my short-yardage running and also because I think it doesn't get much cooler than the 1970s Oakland Raiders. I added New York Jets rookie running back Kevin Long, who will be a nonfactor in 1977 but who rushes for nearly 1,000 yards in 1978.

I traded Theismann for good-not-great wide receiver Reggie Rucker and quarterback Brian Sipe—a pair of real-life Cleveland Browns. Sipe was statistically similar to Theismann but enjoyed a couple of MVP-quality seasons in the early 1980s. He'll be my quarterback of the near future.

My offensive line featured players who were a year away from retirement at offensive tackle (Ralph Neely and Dick Himes) but some solid contributors with future upside at guard (Randy Rasmussen) and center (Carl Mauck). My tight ends were utterly unremarkable (Bob Parris and Andre Tillman), as was most of my secondary. It was going to be a long season, but I was eager to dive in.

I took my lumps. It turns out the old men with impeccable e-mail manners were ruthless on the virtual field. But I discovered a few things that would help me in 1978. I found that I could run the ball without a marquee back and behind some pretty unremarkable linemen. My tailback, Dexter Bussey, was on pace to gain over 1,000 yards before an injury shelved him late in the season. And he spent most of 1977 among the league's top-five rushers. But there was one caveat: I needed a quality blocking back in front of Bussey in order to open holes. In 1977 that role was filled by an aging Larry Csonka, and in 1978 it would be Don Hardeman.

I also discovered that I had a receiver in Reggie Rucker. He led the league in receptions and was responsible for the few "explosion" plays I had in 1977. My linebacker Mark Arneson was among the league's top tacklers, and I got double-digit sack production from Chavous.

I also learned that while I lived by the run, I died by the pass—particularly turnovers from Brian Sipe. And 1977 was an especially brutal interception year for Sipe, which manifested itself in our league. Too many drives were killed by interceptions in the red zone. Adding playmakers for Sipe and building my offensive line would be draft-day priorities.

DRAFT DAY

Draft day in our league actually happens over the course of a few weeks, as each owner/coach has twenty-four hours to make his selection, which is a concession to the fact that we all have jobs, families, and lives that don't revolve around a fetishistic obsession with retro football. And, just as in real football, I had an entire forty-man roster to cultivate on draft day. Our league mandates a certain number of roster cuts, and since it was an expansion year (we would add two 1978 franchises), I had to leave several of my players unprotected. As a result, I would end up turning over half of my roster.

Because I didn't have the absolute worst team in the league (a small point of pride) and managed to win a few games, I would be drafting in the number six slot. In my opinion, there were a handful of truly marquee players in 1978's draft—including defensive end Al "Bubba" Baker; wide receivers Wes Chandler, John Jefferson, and James Lofton; offensive tackle Mike Kenn; and running back Earl Campbell. I decided that I would be happy with either Jefferson or Chandler, but I was really hoping that somehow, some way, Earl Campbell would be there in the six spot. I imagined him fueling my power run game for the few years that he burned bright as an NFL star before injuries and his reckless style took their toll on his body. Even though it's a sim league, I envisioned Campbell providing an "identity" for my offense. Campbell was everything I love in a running back—big, fast, and brutally efficient.

As it turns out, he wasn't there. Campbell went off the board one pick ahead of mine, leaving me with the choice of Chandler or Bubba Baker. It was a tough call. Baker had some incredible sack seasons in the late 1970s, but his production tailed off thereafter. And as players like Mario Williams, Julius Peppers, and even the great J. J. Watt have illustrated, one dominant pass rusher does not a championship defense make. Although passing on Baker would mean that I would have to once again generate a pass rush with smoke and mirrors by committing linebackers to blitz in order to bring pressure. It would be great to have Baker, but he's a luxury I can't afford. Since my offense is closer than my defense to actually being legitimate, I've decided, for better or worse, to focus on making that unit as competitive as possible.

Meanwhile, Chandler was a consistent playmaker through the late 1970s and early 1980s at wide receiver and I certainly needed guys who could catch the ball, as I was down to one receiver again (Rucker).

I got my hands on a rookie-year 1978 tape of Chandler and his New Orleans Saints traveling to Cincinnati to face the Bengals, who were quarterbacked by an old acquaintance from another book, John Reaves. Reaves, a former Florida Gator and first-round draft choice of the Philadelphia Eagles, had, like a number of NFL players in the 1970s, his own battles with substance abuse. He would bounce around with a number of teams before finally finding success in the oddest of places—as a starting quarterback for the USFL's Tampa Bay Bandits, playing for his former college teammate Steve Spurrier. Reaves was filling in for the injured Ken Anderson and would square off against Archie Manning—father, of course, of Peyton and Eli. Manning had the dubious distinction of being an immensely talented pro quarterback who would spend the majority of his career playing for bad teams. Manning was having a great passing year in spite of his team's 1–2 record and certainly benefited from having Chandler on the field.

One apparent oddity in this game was the fact that the Bengals appeared to have no markings of any kind on their helmets. This was before the current tiger stripes, and, while less gaudy, the uniform had a very vanilla "poor-man's Cleveland Browns" look about it. They actually had a barely-discernible-from-TV-distance sticker on the side of their orange helmet that read "BENGALS," but from any distance away it just looked blank. It occurs to me that this would never happen in todays "made for TV" NFL.

The tape would also give me an opportunity to watch one of my linebackers, Jim Merlo, who was a starter for the Saints, as well as one of my former fringe players, Bengals fullback Boobie Clark. On the Bengals' first running play of the game, Merlo made a nice stop on two-time Heisman Trophy winner but pro disappointment Archie Griffin.

Chandler's first touch is on a booming punt by Cincinnati punter Pat McInally, who (1) played collegiately at Harvard, (2) is also a wide receiver, and (3) is white. It's safe to say these are three things you'd never find combined in one wide receiver in today's NFL. Chandler was proof of a paradigm shift that was slowly happening across the league, as the skill positions were slowly adding speed (i.e., black players) across the board. Grinders like Pete Banaszak, Marv Hubbard, and the like were being phased out by 1978, largely never to return again. The league was changing.

Other curiosities: The Bengals started Reggie Williams at linebacker, which is noteworthy both because he also played in the Ivy League (Dartmouth) and because he played so long and so well for the Bengals. He did so rather quietly and for teams that didn't win titles and so has been largely forgotten. This is a shame because Williams was an elite player. One of Cincy's starting safeties is future NFL head coach Dick Jauron. And there is no music in the stadium—either over the public address system or as a part of the game telecast. This is in sharp contrast to today's NFL buildings, where nonstop cacophony is the norm.

The game gives me a chance to appreciate the skills of Bengals big-back Pete Johnson, who is clearly the most talented Bengal back despite the fact that they are committed to Griffin. Johnson is thick, low-slung, and powerful, like an early version of Jerome Bettis.

Oddities:

1. The AstroTurf carpet at Riverfront Stadium had a weird "brushed" pattern to it, which is not unlike the pattern you see in your own carpets at home after running the vacuum sweeper. Being that the playing surface was the same as the indoor/outdoor carpet on your porch, it had to occasionally be cleaned, dried, and disinfected, which was done by a large machine that was a cross between a Zamboni, a vacuum cleaner, and a street sweeper, all of which makes cutting and lining a natural grass field seem really sensible and appealing.

2. Actor Levar Burton was starring in a baseball biopic called *One in a Million: The Ron LeFlore Story* about a player who was signed to the Detroit Tigers while serving time in the Jackson State Penitentiary and playing his first organized baseball in a penal league.

3. New York Yankees owner George Steinbrenner and manager Billy Martin were featured in a Miller Lite ad meant to capitalize on the fact that they were constantly embroiled in conflict and that the former was always firing the latter. The ad made light of this interpersonal dynamic in hopes that you, the consumer, would buy Miller Lite. This, of course, was advertising gold. Nobody sold beer like Miller Lite in the 1970s. Imagine one of today's NFL owners in a beer commercial: Shad Khan? Michael McCaskey? Perhaps Jerry Jones being

jealous of the credit the beer was getting or Daniel Snyder overpaying for a mediocre microbrew?

4. Regarding commercials, I don't understand the logic behind the Michelin Man. He is big and puffy and white yet doesn't appear to be made of tires per se.

5. The league had no particular compunction about limiting helmet-to-helmet hits, and, as such, there were a couple of hellacious shots given and taken in this game. Bengals running back Tony Davis ran a wheel route out of the backfield in the second quarter and was absolutely sent into orbit by New Orleans safety Tommy Myers. He crumpled to the carpet, momentarily unconscious, his arms in the familiar "fencing" pose of the concussion. CBS reruns the play about twenty-five times.

6. Color guy and former Chiefs head coach Hank Stram continually refers to Bengals defensive back Tom Dinkel as "Tinkle." Although he catches himself doing this, he apparently can't stop doing it. There is something almost Joe Pescian about Stram's on-air persona, and I mean that as a compliment. Also, Stram's toupee is epic.

7. Chandler has a sensational fifty-yard kickoff return negated by a clipping penalty. But I've seen enough. He's the best player still available in my draft.

I pulled the trigger on Chandler and then traded backup quarterback Richard Todd (who was also brutal for me in 1977) for defensive tackle Abdul Salaam (a solid but not spectacular starter) and quarterback Bert Jones, whom I acquired primarily because I thought he was cool in the Miller Lite commercials but also because he could give me starter-quality reps as a backup quarterback in the event of a Sipe injury. I had another pick at the end of the first round that I used on playmaking tight end David Hill, who would give me a couple of Pro Bowl–quality seasons (in 1978 and 1979) and play well into the 1980s. With the additions of Chandler and Hill, I infused my offense with a couple of Pro Bowl–caliber playmakers.

With the number six pick in the second round, I grabbed longtime Bengals offensive tackle Mike Wilson, who started opposite Anthony Munoz for over a decade.

Since 1978 was pretty thin in terms of draft talent, the latter rounds were defined by finding the right journeymen to fit my team's system. I grabbed a couple of decent cornerbacks in J. C. Wilson and Curtis Johnson and a third wide receiver in real-life Ram Billy Waddy. And I turned offensive lineman Steve Sylvester into wide receiver/return specialist Billy "White Shoes" Johnson, whom I met when he was in one of his final years in the league as an Indianapolis Colt and I was a hopelessly uncool little kid in Indiana. He let me carry his helmet and shoulder pads at training camp, which I thought, at that time, was the coolest thing that had ever happened to me. All told, my player haul looked like this:

Wes Chandler, wide receiver
Bert Jones, quarterback (via trade—Richard Todd)
Abdul Salaam, defensive tackle (via trade—Richard Todd)
David Hill, tight end
Mike Wilson, offensive tackle
Curtis Johnson, cornerback (via trade—Danny Reece)
Billy Waddy, wide receiver
Barry Bennett, defensive tackle
Bob Glazebrook, safety

Tom Skladany, punter

Frank Corrall, kicker

Lenvil Elliot, running back (he will be my 1979 blocking back)

Art Stringer, linebacker

Billy "White Shoes" Johnson, wide receiver/return specialist

Chandler, Wilson, and Hill will start for me right away and provide a significant infusion on offense, as they're all upgrades over the guys I had in their positions in 1977. And the existence of Waddy and Billy Johnson will allow me to experiment with some three- and four-wide-receiver formations. Journeyman Art Stringer will start for me by default, as will Abdul Salaam and Curtis Johnson. Bennett was a bit of a luxury pick in that he doesn't start being a productive player until the early 1980s but has a nice run of significant seasons at that point.

Through a shadowy Internet figure who plays fast and loose with NFL copyright laws, I managed to obtain a full 1978 telecast of a Chicago Bears–Detroit Lions game. The game featured two mediocre teams with losing records playing a meaningless game, but I couldn't have been more excited to see the old concrete Soldier Field turf and the old concrete columns and removable bleachers in the north end zone.

It is apparent, early on, that there is a natural flow to the game in 1978 that is lacking today. Here are a few differences:

1. Fewer penalties. Given the NFL's current obsession with "player safety," there are an abundance of calls for roughing the passer, targeting, helmet-to-helmet contact,

and unnecessary roughness happening today that weren't there in 1978. It seems like the officials—while a constant story line today—were seldom seen and even less often heard from in the late 1970s. It's super-refreshing to watch several plays unfolding in a row without the intrusion of penalties.

2. Replay. In 1978, the NFL hadn't yet embraced instant replay as a means of perfecting the imperfect. As a result, there were no challenge flags, no mandatory reviews of scoring plays, and no booth reviews in the last two minutes of the half. The result was a product that assumed human error (I can live with that) but that also flowed *much* more smoothly. Calls were made on the field, and the assumption was either that (1) the officials were right or that (2), if they were wrong, nothing could be done about it.

3. More run blocking. NFL linemen in 1978 got into three-point stances on each play and generally drive blocked "downhill," meaning that they fired off the ball and drove opponents. The linemen looked more athletic, less fat, and more aggressive.

4. Sleeves. The jerseys in 1978 looked more like actual jerseys and less like the Spandex, Nike-produced sausage casings that dominate today. Really until a few years ago, teams had individual contracts with individual jersey providers such that each jersey had its own unique look. Jersey homogeneity seemed to enter the league via the Reebok uniform contract in the early 2000s—to the league's detriment. Gone are the Durene jerseys sported by Pittsburgh and Cleveland and the

unique porthole mesh worn by Seattle in the 1980s and 1990s.

5. Arm pads. All linemen and linebackers wore forearm and hand pads that, ostensibly, were a hedge against the skin-destroying AstroTurf of the era but also just made sense given the style of the run blocking and the fact that linebackers in 1978 were doing more than just pursuing bubble screens and dropping into coverage. I'm not sure exactly why the arm pads fell out of fashion, but I suspect that the answer is fashion. They don't look cool.

6. Ron Burgundy–style sideline reporting. In 1978, the vapid sideline hottie hadn't yet become a "thing," but there was still sideline reporting, usually via a guy in a very garish blazer who actually talked about football but also spent a lot of time talking about the "mood" of the sideline. (Example: "There is *no* enthusiasm on the Chicago sideline . . . it's like somebody died over here.") Stay classy, Chicago.

7. Earnest, kick-ass advertising. In 1978, every beer brand had a really great slow ballad written about it—and not in a funny way but rather in a "these people are all sitting on a porch drinking Miller Lite and of course there's a slow song (about the beer) playing in the background" sort of way. And every beer ad that didn't feature a slow, awesome ballad did feature Rodney Dangerfield (even better). The Ford Motor Company seemed to buy at least two-thirds of the advertising slots on the telecast with which to advertise all of their crappy cars. "That looks like a Datsun," said my dad, when the ad for the 1978 Ford Mustang came on. It really was a dreadful era for the domestic car. In the same way that many of

us refuse to acknowledge the existence of *Rocky V*, it's hard not to want to ignore these Ford Mustangs and pretend they never happened.

8. Longer-tenured quarterbacks. Starting Chicago quarterback Bob Avellini was in his fourth season in 1978. Despite a career completion percentage right at 50 percent and a brutal touchdown-to-interception ratio of thirty-three to sixty-nine, Avellini started every game for Chicago in 1976 and 1977 and all but one in 1978, when he threw only five touchdowns and sixteen interceptions, marking the end of his run as the starter. My point, though, is that we live in an era in which teams are bailing on their "franchise" quarterbacks after a season or two (e.g., E. J. Manuel, Blaine Gabbert, Geno Smith, Christian Ponder, etc.). To be fair, some of those guys are actually bad and deserve to be bailed on—but not all of them. The reason for this quick release is, I think, in part because of the constancy of the noise generated by social media and the proliferation and constancy of the regular round-the-clock sports media. ESPN alone is a nonstop multimedia source of noise that is bound to have some degree of influence on NFL decision makers. In 1978, the average Bear fan may have been disgusted with Avellini's performances but had no real outlet for his disgust. Save for a few minutes of coverage on the local news and a short pregame show, there was no during-the-week Chicago Bears coverage for fans to obsess over. Today, fans have more power and influence than ever, which on the surface sounds intriguing but is actually just really loud, shrill, and annoying.

9. A refreshing lack of side story lines. The presentation
   was very straightforward in that it included no camera
   shots of assistant coaches, no dialogue about controver-
   sies or internal bickering, and very few story lines surrounding the head coaches. Alleged defensive genius
   Buddy Ryan was at the helm of a then-underwhelming
   Bear defense, proving that there's a big difference between Jerry Muckensturm, an ancient Doug Buffone,
   and Don Rives (starting 1978 linebacking corps) and
   Mike Singletary, Otis Wilson, and Wilber Marshall
   (starting 1985 linebacking corps). In 1985, Ryan would
   introduce the concept of the televised coaching contro-
   versy, as his soap opera with head coach Mike Ditka
   would run for the duration of the season, culminating in
   both coaches being carried off the field at the end of
   Super Bowl XX. Football would never be the same, as it
   seems like today you can't turn on a game without an in-
   depth meditation on who isn't getting along.[1] Interestingly, in a long November 1984 *Sports Illustrated* essay
   about how to fix the NFL, Paul Zimmerman wrote,
   "Speed up the officials. On an obvious call, let the man
   make his announcement right away, without turning it
   into a production number . . . keep the action cleaner
   from a sound and sight standpoint. Let's have less clut-
   ter on the screen and less jargon and general gab through
   the microphone. . . . Let the action speak."[2] None of that
   has actually happened and has all, in fact, gotten markedly worse.
10. The feature back. Primary Lions runners Dexter Bussey
    and Horace King stayed on the field—the whole game.
    Ditto for Bears superstar Walter Payton, who, in his

fourth season, was really in his prime and was playing at a speed above the rest of his peers. Payton was dynamic. On one second-half play, he lined up at tight end, streaked down the field, and caught a bomb over his shoulder and the very next play carried the ball on a sweep. In today's NFL, the player would have tapped his helmet, indicating that he needed a rest after the long route, and probably wouldn't have carried the ball for the remainder of the drive. Today there are third-down backs, short-yardage backs, change-of-pace backs, and blocking backs. Payton was the best of all of those things in one player.

Speaking of Payton, he was Chicago's entire offense. Their "receiving corps" was comprised of a washed-up ex-Cowboy, Golden Richards, and a little white guy named Steve Schubert, who was actually pretty dynamic, kind of a poor-man's Danny Amendola, who is himself a poor-man's Wes Welker. I just mentioned every white receiver in NFL history in that note, Ed McCaffery notwithstanding. Of Avellini's fifteen completions, seven went to Payton. I know I mentioned it above, but it was a pleasure to have access to a rare, extended look at Payton in his prime. His speed never changed from the first to the fourth quarter. He threw savage lead blocks for backfield mate Roland Harper and even for Avellini, as the Bears were oddly committed to running the kind of quarterback sweep you see drawn up in youth football games. Chicago's offense was laughably simplistic, as you could (seemingly) list the number of formations and plays in their arsenal on the back of a cocktail napkin. And they were notably devoid of talent, Payton and Harper notwithstanding. Interestingly, they managed to grind out a 7–9 record, which was better than the 2014 Chicago squad, which was by comparison laden with talent, including Jay Cutler, Brandon Marshall, Alshon Jeffery, and Martellus Bennett on an offense coached by supposed guru Marc Trestman.

The tape gave me a look at several players who will be significant contributors for me in 1978. I was thoroughly impressed with David Hill, who looks like the kind of field-stretching Antonio Gates–type tight end that is in vogue today. He represented a significant chunk of the Detroit passing game. I was also impressed with Detroit offensive tackle Brad Oates, who will start for me in 1978, and running back Bussey, who was exactly what I thought he was—a grinder who hit the hole hard, didn't dance, and got the most out of his blocks. I wanted to upgrade the running back position in the off-season, but the 1978 draft provided slim pickings at that position. I will roll into the season with Bussey and Kevin Long, who will, in actuality, probably look a lot like the Bussey–Horace King tandem I just watched. Bubba Baker was indeed a freaky-good defensive end, and I had more than a moment of regret that I didn't draft him. Time will tell.

More than anything, though, the tape was just a pleasure. It was fun to watch my dad watching "his" NFL and enjoying the era. And it was fun to watch an NFL that was less painfully self-aware and self-obsessed than today's league, which seems so preoccupied with image and perception on both an individual (player) and a corporate (league) level. The graphics were primitive, the intro/outro music was dumb and meaningless, but it was like watching a football game rather than watching a production of a football game.

4

CARL MAUCK

We Had More Fun Back Then

Carl Mauck is maybe the most grizzled guy I've ever spoken with in person. The former Houston Oilers center—my center in the 1978 sim league—has the kind of gravelly, raspy voice befitting of an ex–offensive lineman, ex-coach. He is John Madden meets Dan Jenkins meets Sam Elliot. He is scotch with a side of cigarettes. Mauck played thirteen NFL seasons with four different teams and then served as an offensive-line coach for several more. Still, he has trouble understanding why I want to talk with him about a computerized sim league organized by old men.

"How in the hell did you get stuck with my ass?" says Mauck after I explain that he is my starting center. I imagine him punctuating sentences with a stream of tobacco juice hitting the bottom of a Styrofoam cup. I explain to Mauck that he was my dad's favorite center in the 1970s, and therefore I made it a goal to place him on my team. Both his voice and his delivery are pure "coach."

"Was he nice?" asked my son after the interview. I scratched my head and thought for a minute.

"He was kind of coach-nice," I explained. "Meaning mean-nice. He was grizzled. He's the kind of guy you don't want to be on the wrong side of." In that, it may have been the most enjoyable interview I've ever had, starting with Mauck's meditation on how social media is horseshit.

"You can take social media and stick it right up your ass," he explains. "They don't know jack shit"—"they being sideline reporters and television talking heads not named John Madden. "Gimme Madden any day," he says. "At least he knows the game." What Mauck is bemoaning is a nonstop river of NFL-related information that flows out of televisions, radios, computers, tablets, and smart phones that, theoretically, may be construed as good by an ex-player and ex-coach like Mauck. Except that it isn't. More football coverage doesn't necessarily mean better football coverage.

It becomes clear, though, that what Mauck enjoys most is talking about football and, specifically, offensive-line play.

"When you're in a spread offense, all you do is pass protect and zone block," he says of college spread schemes and their failure to create pro-ready linemen. "A lot of these kids have never been in a three-point stance. They don't pull, they don't trap, and they don't know pocket [pass protection] schemes. The pros still operate primarily out of a two-back offense."

I ask Mauck what he looks for when scouting draft-eligible linemen.

"They've gotta have 'that' mentality," he says. "They've gotta be offensive linemen with a defensive line mentality. They've gotta want to dish out punishment. The best center I ever coached was a guy named Courtney Hall, who graduated from Rice University at age twenty. He was a small guy, about 6′3″ and 260. He had great, quick hands. He was very quick on his feet and smart. He even learned how to read coverages and tell where the blitzers were coming from. And he was tough enough.

"My best guard was Eric Moten out of Michigan State. He was about 6′4″ and 295. Boy, he was a tough bastard. He had great strength, and he would strike your ass! He got hurt when we were trying to throw the damn ball when the damn game was over. We should have just run out the clock. Anyway, a guy went inside on him, and he got knocked into the quarterback's leg. He tore a ligament and ended up with a drop foot, which meant that he couldn't really lift up his foot. He never really recovered and was never the same. If he had stayed healthy, he would have been in the Hall of Fame.

"My other guard is Ruben Brown, who I coached with the Buffalo Bills. He was strong, strong, strong. He could run block and pass protect. He'll be in the Hall of Fame. And my tackle is a guy named Stan Brock, who I coached twice. I coached him for four years in New Orleans and three in San Diego. He was a big strong son of a bitch at 6′7″ and 300 pounds. And he could move."

When talk turns to physical players, we naturally talk about Mauck's Hall of Fame teammate with the Oilers, Earl Campbell. Campbell, a compact 5′11″ and 232, would be my most coveted player in the 1978 sim draft, and all of my "don't draft a running back high" sensibilities would fly out the window. He was perhaps the most physically dominant and brutal running back to ever play the game, which no doubt took a great toll on Campbell himself. I ask Mauck what it was like to block for the great runner.

"Want to know what it sounds like?" he asks. "Get about five feet from the damn railroad tracks and close your eyes. Then wait for the train to come through. If you're on the tracks when that son of a bitch came through the hole, he'd run your ass over. He was big, strong, and fast enough to go the distance. He went eighty damn yards, around the horn, to beat the Miami Dolphins in a Monday Night Football game."

Frank Gifford called the game "the most exciting we've ever had," and then–Oilers head coach Bum Phillips said "it was like a college crowd." Campbell was sensational. He scored four times, including the run Mauck references, in which he took a toss to the short side of the field and used his pure speed to outrace Miami's pursuit to the corner and then beat them the rest of the way. It was truly remarkable to see a man his size move that quickly. It is reminiscent of Bo Jackson's Monday Night beating of Brian Bosworth and the Seattle Seahawks.

"We were playing the Raiders," Mauck remembers. "We were down on the goal line, and Earl hit their safety, Jack Tatum, at the one-yard line. It sounded like a cannon went off. Tatum was a tough son of a bitch too. He played for us at the end of his career."

Mauck is clearly nostalgic for the way things were. It's hard to blame him. Today's game is, in many ways, unrecognizable.

"We've got a bunch of thugs playing now," he says. "The kinds of guys who beat up women. It's a shame. It's embarrassing. They've got a pocket full of money and think they can do anything they want.

"And there's not many colorful characters anymore. These kids play their game and then go home in a suit and tie. My first six years in the league, I made $96,000—total. But I think we had more fun. We were together more. That's what happens when you spend a long time with the same team. These kids play a few years and then, if they're lucky, get a truckload of money to go play someplace else. They never develop any friendships."

Mauck leaves with an exhortation to the author to clean up his language. "Take out the f-words," he says. "You can leave the 'shits' and 'damns' in there, but no f-words."

"I will," I assure him.

"Good, because if you don't, you're gonna have a problem."

1978—WEEK ONE: IMPROVED BUT STILL OVERMATCHED

I started the 1978 sim season against my league's defending NFC champion—the Midway Monsters. The Monsters featured a Hall of Fame–caliber squad whose strength was anchored in its offensive and defensive lines—in short, the kind of team I would like to build. His offensive line boasts Hall of Famer John Hannah and his old New England teammate Leon Gray—both rated "10s" for 1978. Defensively, he was even stronger, starting Alan Page, Dave Butz, Fred Dean, and John Matuszak up front, to go with a peaking Randy Gradishar and a still-explosive Thomas "Hollywood" Henderson at linebacker. His starting safeties were 1985 Bear stalwart Gary Fencik and Raiders star Jack Tatum.

While I would like, in theory, to build through the draft, I had to add players just to reach a baseline of competitiveness for 1978. In Washington Redskins/Daniel Snyder fashion, I traded away a draft choice for an aging but still great cornerback, Roger Wehrli, and did the same for a less great defensive end in Cedric Hardman. Oddly, I was feeling the pressure to win immediately, which is something that is talked about often in today's NFL. I hate losing so much, even in pretend football, that I was willing to begin Snydering my draft choices away in exchange for bodies that would make me more competitive immediately. I have a massive rebuild on my hands, and the work of cultivating an entire roster has given me newfound respect for real NFL personnel men.

Still, my roster pales by comparison to Midway's, and my first big mistake was starting quarterback Brian Sipe over the far better Bert Jones, whom I'd acquired in an off-season trade. Jones, the son of former Cleveland Browns running back Dub Jones, was a consensus All-American at LSU and was chosen in the first round of the 1973 NFL Draft by the Baltimore Colts. He is the personification of the "prototype" NFL quarterback. With Jones in the lineup from 1975 to 1977, the Colts enjoyed three consecutive AFC East titles. With Jones sidelined due to a shoulder injury for most of 1978–1979, the Colts fell to last in the AFC East. I hope this isn't a harbinger of things to come for my club.

Former New York Giants general manager Ernie Acorsi once said of Jones that if he'd played under different circumstances, he "probably would have been the greatest player ever." Hopefully, my sim team will provide that different circumstance, though with the sim engine's loyalty to maintaining real-life narratives, I don't know how long I'll have him in 1978.

My logic in going with Sipe initially was that Sipe's numbers were solid in 1978, and Jones played only three games that season. However, I was overlooking the simple and obvious truth that Jones had a bigger arm, could run (helpful given my mediocre offensive line), and was way better. I learned the hard way. Sipe started the game five for fifteen for fifty-nine yards and his usual interception—replicating the same Geno Smith–like numbers that he posted in 1977. I replaced him in the third quarter with Jones, who immediately found my new receiving talent (Wes Chandler and David Hill) and moved our team up and down the imaginary Soldier Field carpet for a pair of touchdowns.

Chandler, a rookie who really doesn't begin to "peak" until 1979 and the early 1980s, caught seven balls for sixty-five yards. Last sim season's league-leading receiver, Reggie Rucker, chipped in forty-five yards and a score, while my other first-round draft acquisition, Hill, had three catches for forty-nine yards. These players allowed me to keep the game respectable when I was incredibly overmatched on paper.

Even though my 1977 record didn't necessarily show it, I learned how to keep games close and respectable with a bad team. This was probably a function, at some level, of playing on so many bad teams as a player. I wanted to avoid frustrating blowouts, so I learned to mask my defensive talent drain with exotic and constant blitzes, which is a technique still employed by talent-challenged defenses today. I was able to do the same thing against Midway, managing to contain quarterback Kenny Stabler to some degree by blitzing him relentlessly. I tried to make the most of Wehrli, isolating him on Midway's best receiver. As a result, most of their points came off my turnovers—the previously mentioned Sipe pick and an unfathomable three fumbles by the usually sure-handed Dexter Bussey. I even had to resort to a gimmicky onside kick in the third quarter to steal another possession.

I may have also handed the reins to the team to my twelve-year-old son and assistant coach Tristan for a little while in the third quarter, as I was exasperated with Sipe's ineptitude and Bussey's fumbling. I was reminded (by him) that NFL coaches don't have the option of sulking off to the living room to read a book for a few minutes during game action. Tristan, who tends to be a little more cavalier in his play calling, led a scoring drive that had us high-fiving in the kitchen. What was most encouraging was our ability to throw downfield in a way we never could in 1977, when our offense lacked receivers and a big-armed quarterback.

The final was a respectable 27–14, Midway. His club rushed for over 200 yards, and my defense was powerless to stop it. This, as it turned out, was the story of the game. Midway won in exactly the fashion I would like to win these games someday—on the efforts of superior defense and a sound running game.

5

A LONG HANDOFF

The Death of the Pro-Style Offense
(and Maybe Also the Death of
the Franchise Quarterback)

I wrote this, about the spread offense, in 2008:

My dad called me midway through the third quarter of the Michigan–Ohio State blowout yesterday to say that "If Michigan runs that little bubble screen one more time, I'm going to claw my eyes out." That little bubble screen is, of course, a staple of the spread scheme, and either not completing it or completing it for a gain of minus two yards seemed to be the reason for many of the second- and third-and-longs Michigan found itself in on Saturday. All spread teams run this play into the ground, with the logic that it "forces the defense to defend the whole field," which is true, in theory, but in reality there's usually a good cornerback a few yards away who has looked at the play about a million times in the film room and knows exactly what to do with it. If I had more time, I would pick a program—say, Michigan—and chart the percentage of times this play worked successfully. I bet it would be low:

1. The spread-option offense doesn't work without the threat of a running quarterback. Every successful spread-option team in recent history had a better-than-average runner at quarterback: Pat White, Tim Tebow, Vince Young, the kid from Appalachian State, Dennis Dixon, Dan LeFevour, Juice Williams, and so on. A dynamic runner at quarterback can make this a viable college offense. Michigan does not have a dynamic runner.

2. The spread-option offense produces crappy NFL quarterbacks. The rise of the spread in college football could have something to do with the dearth of good quarterbacking at the NFL level these days, where you can't line up in four wides and run your quarterback every other play without getting him killed. Vince Young is a case in point, as he's currently completing what seems like about 30 percent of his passes on the pro level and hasn't even distinguished himself as a runner. Another case is Alex Smith, who in the second iteration of his pro career has turned himself into a viable NFL starter. Not spectacular but solid. Smith is a former first-overall pick who was overdrafted. In fact, besides Young, I am hard pressed at the moment to name one better-than-average NFL starter who came from a spread scheme in college. Sam Bradford played in one at Oklahoma, and he has struggled at the pro level.

3. One would assume that if the spread produces crappy NFL quarterbacks, the same will prove to be true of

running backs. Most of the young runners who have had success recently at the pro level—guys like Adrian Peterson, Joseph Addai, Marion Barber, and Marshawn Lynch—have come from pro-style college offenses. This doesn't bode well for Rashard Mendenhall and Jonathan Stewart—two products of spread offenses.

4. The spread produces running plays that go east to west instead of north to south. If the running back starts with any momentum at all, it's lateral momentum, which makes it difficult for him to square his shoulders to the line of scrimmage. Again, ideally, in this offense you have a Pat White or a Tim Tebow pitching the ball a few yards downfield after getting the corner. As for Michigan, it's sad to see talented fullbacks like Mark Moundrous and Vince Helmuth rotting on the bench and talented tailbacks like Sam McGuffie and Brandon Minor not running behind said fullbacks.

5. There's a difference between the spread option and what June Jones ran with great success at Hawaii. Jones was one of the early adopters of the whole run-and-shoot phenomenon in the late 1980s (e.g., Mouse Davis)—an offense that employs four- and five-wide sets and lots of small, slot-type receivers who modify their routes based on defensive formations. The run-and-shoot is a viable offense because it operates free of the pretense of a running game in most cases (e.g., the huge numbers put up by Colt Brennan and, before him, Timmy Chang). The run-and-shoot also doesn't require an especially nifty quarterback.

ENDANGERED SPECIES AND THE SPREAD

Since I wrote that meditation on the spread in 2008, the offense has continued to proliferate at the high school and college levels. Another reason for the death of the franchise quarterback is the fact that the NFL's de facto farm system—bigtime college football—is moving away from "pro-style" offenses en masse. If you like watching fullbacks, good luck finding one on television on a Saturday afternoon, unless you happen to catch the LSU–Alabama game, which is my Super Bowl because both teams use fullbacks and run pro-style schemes (though Alabama has crept closer and closer to bubble-screen hell since they hired Lane Kiffin). Stanford, Arkansas, and Georgia Tech are a few of the remaining teams that don't operate out of a primarily spread scheme. For the first time in the history of its long relationship with college football, college programs are failing to produce players who can do the things that NFL offenses will ask them to do.

The Blocking Tight End

Gone are the days of players like Zeke Mowatt and Kyle Brady—big-bodied tight ends who were great in-line blockers and whose presence fueled great running games. They have been replaced by a bevy of former basketball players and "slot" tight ends who are, to be fair, athletically intriguing but who are also (to be fair again) nonexistent blockers.

The 2014 Minnesota–Ohio State tape is a great opportunity to view a couple of the 2015 draft's top tight end prospects. Both Jeff Heuerman (Ohio State) and Maxx Williams play in college-style shotgun offenses, but both occasionally do pro-style things and provide more versatility than 2014's top-drafted tight end, Eric Ebron (Detroit Lions), who operated almost exclusively as a slot receiver in college and was drafted on the strength of his impressive 4.5-second forty-yard dash at the NFL Scouting Combine. Ebron struggled to adjust to pro football as a rookie and failed to make a significant impact, catching only twenty-five passes for 248 yards and one touchdown.

Williams is widely considered the best tight end in college football. He has good size, at 6'4" and 250 pounds, and is a surprisingly willing and occasionally capable blocker. However, both he and Heurmann are "position" blockers, meaning that they rarely have the strength or the inclination to try to drive a defender off the ball. Both are often on the move from slot or wing alignments. What sets Williams apart is his aptitude and involvement in the pass game. Williams was a big part of Minnesota's passing game as a collegian, snagging thirty-six passes for 569 yards and eight scores as a redshirt sophomore. A better way to say it would be that he was Minnesota's *only* significant passing target. Williams is projected to be drafted in the first round and will probably go there, but is he worth that kind of investment?

Contrast these players with Florida State's Nick O'Leary, who, of all the top tight end prospects, does the most pro-style things in his multiple college offense. He was a four-year contributor and had more catches this season than Williams. He is 6'3" and 247, so his chief transgressions seem to be that he is an inch shorter and three pounds lighter than Williams. Such is the strange world of football scouting. The 2014 Florida State–Syracuse film reveals a tight end who lines up in a three-point stance and on the line of scrimmage far more often than Williams or Heuerman. While Williams was his team's *only* receiving threat, O'Leary was on an offense full of five-star playmakers and was still ultra-involved as quarterback Jameis Winston's security blanket. Against Syracuse, he got open on short and intermediate routes, running primarily from the line of scrimmage. Again, a pro-style experience. In the run game, O'Leary was especially adept at climbing upfield and blocking linebackers at the second level.

One of the most successful rookie tight ends in recent history has been Zach Ertz out of Stanford, which runs a pro-style offense. In that offense, Ertz was asked to line up in a three-point stance on the line of scrimmage and do the types of things that tight ends traditionally do, including blocking at the point of attack. While at Stanford, he developed into a legitimate pass-game weapon as well, catching an astonishing sixty-nine passes for 898 yards and six scores. He fell into the second round, where he was a steal at the thirty-fifth-overall spot. Ertz caught fifty-eight passes for 702 yards and three touchdowns as a Philadelphia Eagle in 2014. This puts Maxx Williams's campaign for top tight end in the 2015 draft into sharper focus. He has caught markedly fewer balls and done less pro-style blocking in a less conventional offense, which begs the question: Why do we feel the need to "manufacture" first-round prospects at a given position when, clearly, those prospects sometimes don't exist? A simple answer is that there are still thirty-two teams that will make first-round selections and, chances are, one of those teams will need a tight end.

Ertz's predecessor at Stanford, Coby Fleener, caught fifty-two passes in 2014 and fifty-one in 2013, as Stanford has developed a recent reputation for producing pro-ready tight ends. Whereas NFL teams had the luxury of choosing a tight end from a cadre of schools two decades ago, the landscape has changed considerably. Teams seem to either target pro-ready prospects from pro-style schools or select a player like New Orleans Saint Jimmy Graham, who offers freakish pass-receiving skill sets but absolutely nothing as a blocker in the run game.

The Run-Blocking Lineman

There were sixty-eight offensive linemen drafted in the first two rounds of the NFL Draft between 2009 and 2015. Of those, twenty were selected from schools that still run pro-style offensive schemes. And while it's possible to find pass rushers from a variety of places based on their measurables and college production, it's tougher to project offensive line-men, although as with quarterbacks and tight ends, it seems to make sense to make an investment of this magnitude on a player with experience in a pro-style system.

To wit: Alabama has five players on the list, all of whom have been relatively successful at the pro level. Iowa, long a bastion of offensive-line talent ready for pro-style systems, has put a pair of first-round tackles into the league during our time frame in Reilly Reiff and Bryan Bulaga. Another pro-style hotbed, Wisconsin, has had four players drafted in the first or second round during the study period, including Pro Bowl center Travis Frederick. USC has placed three players, including two-time Pro Bowler and one-time All-Pro tackle Tyron Smith. The Dallas Cowboys have been especially adept at mining these "pipeline" programs—nabbing both Smith and Frederick in the study period and riding them to a divisional playoff appearance and record-setting year for running back DeMarco Murray in 2014.

Perhaps what's more interesting to note is what has happened when teams have strayed away from pro-style schools and invested high picks on offensive linemen, no doubt wooed by enticing height/weight/speed combinations and impressive Combine numbers. The draft's three most significant offensive-line busts over the past five years have been offensive tackles Jason Smith (Baylor), Luke Joeckel (Texas A&M), and Eric Fisher (Central Michigan). Smith and Joeckel played exclusively in spread systems in college, while Fisher played in a pro-style offense for head coach Dan Enos at Central Michigan.

I broke down Joeckel's 2012 college tape against LSU for the express purpose of seeing how many plays Joeckel ran out of a two-point stance and how many he ran out of a three-point. In the 24–19 loss to the LSU Tigers, Texas A&M ran a total of seventy-nine offensive plays. Seventy-eight of those plays came from the shotgun, and in all of those plays, Joeckel was lined up in a two-point stance. To be fair, there are many NFL offenses that incorporate a lot of shotgun plays. There are NFL teams that use the shotgun on over half of their offensive snaps. Still, there is the matter of the other snaps.

The tape revealed that Joeckel was proficient at pass protection and kick-stepping out of a two-point stance but that, in what little run blocking was required of him, he was often asked only to climb to the next level to shield or "body position" a scraping linebacker. Joeckel was almost never asked to zone block or move a defender. And while Joeckel was praised for his pass blocking and for the number of sacks he didn't give up, that can be deceiving too, as he was playing in an offense that did precious little in the way of long-developing pass plays. Spread offenses get the ball out quick, and as a result, Joeckel didn't have to do much to stymie a pass rusher like Barkevious Mingo against LSU. As is (in part) the point of the spread, Mingo was neutralized, but not primarily because of Joeckel's greatness.

Another Joeckel exposure was Texas A&M's 2012 game against Alabama. Again, I broke down each offensive snap and found that out of sixty-six total offensive snaps, Joeckel was in a two-point stance for sixty-three of them. A&M's running game consisted almost entirely of draw plays out of the shotgun and designed Johnny Manziel runs. Joeckel struggled in this game against Alabama's Adrian Hubbard, who went undrafted in the 2014 draft but was signed by Green Bay as a free agent and is currently on their roster. Hubbard, at 6'6" and 257, seemed to bother Joeckel with his burst and length, as the elite tackle was beaten around the corner twice.

Hubbard's story is an interesting departure. He led Alabama in sacks, tackles for loss, and forced fumbles in 2012. At the 2014 NFL Scouting Combine, Hubbard ran a very respectable 4.69-second forty-yard dash, which put him just over a tenth of a second slower than first-overall draft choice Jadeveon Clowney. Hubbard vertical jumped 38.5 inches, which was a full inch better than Clowney. His physical dimensions are very similar, as Clowney was a little shorter at 6'5" but a little heavier, weighing in at 266 at the Combine. The "negatives" on Hubbard's NFL.com Combine Profile read, "Too often disappears for stretches" and "Has a quirky personality . . . carries a sense of entitlement."[1] These things could have easily been written for Clowney. Yet Clowney is the first-overall pick, and Hubbard goes undrafted. To me, his performance against Joeckel in 2012 was impressive and telling. And Joeckel's lack of pro-style experiences should have been a major red flag. Why would we expect Joeckel to be able to immediately run NFL-type plays if he never ran them at the college level? And why would you invest a top-five pick in a player who isn't realistically ready to contribute?

By contrast, former USC tackle Tyron Smith came out of college ready to contribute immediately in a run-oriented pro-style system. Drafted ninth overall by the Dallas Cowboys, Smith entered the draft at just twenty years of age after his junior season. I evaluated Smith's 2010 tape against Virginia, and it revealed a much more balanced prospect. Of Smith's thirty-three plays, he was in a two-point stance for sixteen of them and a three-point stance for seventeen, more closely mimicking the experience he would soon have at the pro level. Smith was asked to do more in his offense than was Joeckel. He showed cut-block proficiency on quick passes as well as the ability to kick and slide with outside pass rushers. In the run game, he was drive blocking defenders as well as position blocking and climbing to the next level to block linebackers. Like Joeckel, he possessed elite size at 6'5" and 307, almost identical to Joeckel's 6'6" and 306. However, he has made a much more successful transition to the pro game.

A recent offensive tackle prospect who has fallen in between Joeckel's struggles and Smith's runaway successes has been Riley Reiff out of Iowa, which is another "pipeline" pro-style program. Reiff has been a starter and solid contributor for the Detroit Lions but has not yet made a Pro Bowl. Similar to Joeckel and Smith, he had ideal size coming out of Iowa at 6'6" and 313.

I studied Reiff's 2011 tape against Nebraska, and, like Smith, he was asked to do a variety of things in his offense. He was in a two-point stance on twenty-two of his plays and in a three-point stance for twenty-three. He showed an ability to cut, drive, and position block as well as some pulling and trapping that Smith wasn't asked to do at USC. It was an extremely clean and mistake-free game for Reiff, and I can see why the Lions were eager to use a first-round selection on him.

The Run-Plugging Mike Linebacker

The proliferation of the spread at the college level has made its mark on defenses as well. Recently, in a fit of nostalgia, I purchased and watched the 1985 Orange Bowl, in which the Brian Bosworth–led Oklahoma Sooners beat the Shane Conlan–led Penn State Nittany Lions. Both of those players were inside linebackers, and both were the stars of their respective teams. College football, in 1985, was a far different animal. Penn State ran a very conservative pro-style offense that leaned heavily on the run and play-action passing. Oklahoma ran a wishbone, offensively, in addition to a lot of classic power/lead-type plays. The result was a linebacker's dream—a game that featured collisions between fullbacks and "mike" backers.

"This game is a bloodbath," I kept saying to my father as we watched collision after collision between big-shoulder-padded players whose uniforms were dirty and torn by the end of the contest. The action in this game was purely "north and south" as players and teams moved vertically at one another rather than laterally.

This statistical project—looking at players as numbers and trying to find interesting trends inside the numbers—tends to tamp down the violence that actually exists in college and pro football. "I'd like to think of myself as a gentle person," said former Packers and Colts center Bill Curry in George Plimpton's *Mad Ducks and Bears.* "But I am violent. You couldn't be a lineman in pro football and not be violent. Everyone has this same facet somewhere in their personality. It's often exposed—the player in a controlled situation venting his hostility on the field, and the fan up in the stands with his yelling doing the same thing . . . and for both of them the effect is cathartic."

As collegiate offensive philosophies have changed, the game has become less violent.

Today's college linebacker, by and large, is a laterally moving player whose first steps are often outside to chase bubble screens or jet sweeps. As a result, the places where NFL teams can find pro-ready linebackers are fewer and far between. To wit: Between 2009 and 2014, there were 179 linebackers drafted. As of February 2015, there are 145 players on that list still drawing an NFL paycheck, which is a pretty astonishing number. That said, it's interesting to see where the successful inside linebackers come from. USC has produced four starting NFL inside linebackers in this period, including Rey Maualuga and Brian Cushing (with an astonishing seven total linebackers on the list). Alabama has put five linebackers on the list—only one of whom (Courtney Upshaw) plays exclusively outside. Its inside linebacking products, including C. J. Mosley, Donta'a Hightower, and Rolando McClain, have been outstanding. Something those Alabama linebackers all share in common is their stature—they are all over 6'2" and over 250 pounds with the exception of C. J. Mosley (234). This is proof that Alabama recruits and produces linebackers with the skill sets to stop SEC pro-style offenses at LSU, Arkansas, and Georgia. These skill sets translate very well to the pro level.

Bastions of the pro-style offense—Iowa and LSU—each put four linebackers on the list. The NFL's best inside linebacker over the past few years—Carolina's Luke Kuechly—came from a Boston College program that runs a pro-style offense. The logic here is that the pro-style linebackers see things in practice each week, each spring, and each preseason for four years, helping them ease the transition to the pro level. In the same way that playing quarterback in a spread-dominated scheme is basically a different job description, the same holds true for linebackers to some degree. A linebacker from the MAC—where nearly every team runs a spread offense—will have a tougher transition than an SEC linebacker who stills sees a lot of pro-style offenses week in and week out.

1978 WEEK TWO: BREAKTHROUGH

Me: "Hello, this is Ted Kluck, Tristan's father. I'm going to need to pull him out of school a few minutes early this afternoon."

Receptionist at Tristan's school: "For what purpose?"

Me: "He has an appointment."

His appointment, of course, was his role as my defensive coordinator and the fact that my online opponent could play only during a time that would overlap with the last twenty minutes of school. I rationalized this away by telling myself that the last twenty minutes of school was a waste of time anyway and that I wouldn't make a habit out of this. I think I might be a terrible father.

Week Two saw my sim Lions hosting the Montana Grizzlies, led by a bunch of guys whose best football was going to be ahead of them. The Grizzlies sole 1978 stud was wide receiver James Lofton, who after Week One was leading the league in receptions (ten) and yards (134). My high-priced corner, Roger Wehrli, would need to come through big time. I decided before the game that I would double-team Lofton on every defensive snap, daring the opposing coach to beat me in other ways. Midweek, I traded for aging safety Paul Krause to take the place of Tim Gray, who was banged up last week.

My Lofton bracket seemed to work, as did my other key off-season acquisition, defensive end Cedric Hardman, who had thirteen sacks in the real 1978 and whom I was counting on to generate a pass rush in sim 1978. He had a sack and forced fumble for me against Montana, giving me the unique pleasure of having my off-season spending spree at least momentarily justified, as both Hardman and Wehrli had great games (after doing basically nothing last week). I also got a couple of sacks from inside linebacker Bob Horn in my blitz-heavy defensive scheme. Still troubling, however, is my lack of run defense, as my front seven, in spite of the Hardman acquisition, is still pretty mediocre. Equally mediocre Montana runners Mike Hogan and Hank Bauer still picked up chunks of yardage on the ground.

My starting wideouts—Rucker and Chandler—were better than Montana's corners, Neal Colzie and Clarence Chapman, and I moved my tight end, David Hill, around the field in order to create one-on-one matchups for Wes Chandler, who responded with a huge day—catching ten balls for well over 100 yards and a score.

Montana got a valiant effort out of future stud linebacker Kim Bokamper, but it wasn't enough to shut down Dexter Bussey (166 yards), Kevin Long (forty-one yards), and the rest of my rushing attack, which operates behind the lead blocking of fullback Don Hardeman.

I was most pleased with Bert Jones, however, who continued his efficient ways, passing for over 200 yards and, most importantly, not turning the ball over.

6

AND TWO OF THEM ARE BAD

Pass Attempts, Rush Attempts,
and Offensive Success

The inaugural NFL Free Agent Combine ended last night and
included some interesting names, including former first-round
draft choices in Felix Jones and Brady Quinn. Jones is an
interesting case in that he was the twenty-second-overall pick
in the 2008 NFL Draft and had a career per-carry average of
4.7 yards over six seasons with the Dallas Cowboys, in which
he was really never given an opportunity to be the featured
guy, as he was always sharing carries with other backs, like
Marion Barber and, later, DeMarco Murray. So, despite his
pedigree and relative lack of "mileage," Jones found himself
out of the league in 2014 and in Phoenix for the Veteran
Combine, where he ran a disappointing 4.79-second forty-yard
dash. Interestingly, none of the other running backs at the
Veteran Combine ran fast either. Former Illinois standout and
Detroit Lions draft choice Mikel Leshoure ran 4.75, and former NFL power back Michael Bush, always a personal favor-

ite of the author, ran 4.96 and said, immediately following, "There you go. There goes my career."

The fact that all these backs were out of football, on the market, and reduced to running timed forties in a made-for-television spectacle at this stage of their football lives all speaks to the pass-obsessed NFL, where the running back has been summarily dismissed in most cases. It also makes you wonder how important the forty-yard dash ever was as well as the reliability of the timing mechanisms. If Jones can be considered a "burner," coming out of Arkansas running a 4.47, and then show up a few years later running slower than most linemen, it does bring the whole process into question. The fact of the matter is that over his career, Jones did what he was paid to do, which is run the ball for over four yards per carry. This in a league where both Trent Richardson and his career 3.3-yards-per-carry average and Darren McFadden and his 3.3-yard average over the past three seasons are gainfully employed. Some things just don't make sense.

What also doesn't seem to make sense is the league's obsession with the passing game when statistics seem to indicate that the best teams run the football. "You can't win in this league without an elite quarterback," said draft guru Mel Kiper Jr. on a recent episode of the *Dari and Mel* podcast, of which I am a fan and regular listener. Kiper is knowledgeable and, more importantly, entertaining in an entertainment business. Yet his statement gave me pause.

In 2014, six of the league's worst teams were Oakland, Tampa Bay, Chicago, Tennessee, Jacksonville, and Atlanta. Of that list, Oakland and Jacksonville were expected to be bad in part because they are always bad but also because both were breaking in rookie "franchise" quarterbacks in Derek Carr and

Blake Bortles, respectively. So they can be shown some grace. More distressing were the 2014 Bears and Falcons. The teams shared some similarities. The Bears started the highest-priced quarterback in the league in Jay Cutler—a player long considered "elite." The Falcons offense was led by quarterback Matt Ryan, considered one of the brightest young quarterbacking stars in the league. Both teams had pairs of elite receivers— Roddy White and Julio Jones in Atlanta and Brandon Marshall and Alshon Jeffery in Chicago. Incidentally, Marshall, who has nearly 10,000 receiving yards and has been to five Pro Bowls, was ranked thirty-first among draftable wide receivers by *Pro Football Weekly* in 2006 and was unranked by *The Sporting News*.

What all six bad teams share in common is that they were the last six teams in the league in rush attempts per game. Now, admittedly, this could be a function of falling behind in many games and then having to pass in order to catch up. But some of the teams on that list either invested heavily in their running attacks (Tennessee) or had elite backs on their roster (Matt Forte in Chicago). So why weren't they running the ball?

More tellingly, five of those six teams *also* led the league in team interceptions thrown per game. So there seems to be a correlation between not running the ball and throwing interceptions. Interceptions, as we know, kill drives. And dead drives kill offenses. Ideally, you want the onus of stopping drives on the defense, not on your offense's propensity for turning the ball over. I've learned this the hard way in my sim league, where, more often than not, my drives end on Brian Sipe interceptions. It follows that you're not throwing interceptions (and not killing drives) if you're running the football a lot and running it well. Legendary Ohio State head coach Woody Hayes famously said, "When you pass, only three things can happen, and two of them [sacks and interceptions] are bad."

Football Outsiders 2014 Drive Data bears this out. Dallas, with its renewed emphasis on the run, was second in the league in touchdowns-per-drive percentage (.312) and had the third-lowest percentage of dreaded three-and-outs in the league (.165). What coaching in the sim league has taught me is that good teams don't end their own drives. We can't always control how good the other team's defense is in relationship to our offense, but we can control (to some degree through play calling) how often we put our drives at risk.

Houston, Seattle, the New York Jets, and Dallas led the league, in that order, in rush attempts. Of those teams, the Texans and Jets were bad. They probably ran the ball because they had few other options given their dearth of quarterbacking talent. But the Seahawks and Cowboys were very good. Seattle came within a play of back-to-back Super Bowl titles, and the Cowboys were a bad call away from advancing to the NFC Championship game. The Cowboys have an expensive star quarterback in Tony Romo and the league's best wide receiver in Dez Bryant. Still, they ran the football. Even a team that is perceived as a pass-first offense, New England, was in the top half of the league in rush attempts despite lacking a "feature" running back. And even Chip Kelly's spread attack—perceived as pass happy—averaged 29.8 rush attempts per game.

But one year and one statistic do not a trend make. Interestingly, of the NFL's ten leaders in rushing *yards* per game, six of those teams made the playoffs. The league's top ten in passing yards per game? Only four of those clubs made the playoffs, and the list was populated with disappointments like the Falcons (6–10), Giants (6–10), and Saints (7–9), all of whom threw for a lot of yards but lost a lot of football games. All three of those teams, it could be noted, have elite and quantifiably great quarterbacks.

The rush-attempts statistic was even more telling in 2013, when the league's elite teams were among its leaders in rush attempts. All four of the league's representatives in each conference's championship game were among the top ten in the league in rush attempts. Of the league's top ten teams in rushing attempts, only the Bills and Jets didn't make the playoffs. And the teams at the bottom of the rush-attempts metric were also, by and large, the teams at the bottom of the league's standings, including the Browns (4–12), Jaguars (4–12), and Falcons (4–12).

What's interesting is that the elite teams in 2013 that were running the ball a lot weren't even necessarily running it especially well. For example, Seattle averaged 4.3 yards per rush attempt, which was only twelfth best in the league, and Denver averaged 4.0 yards per attempt, which was good enough for twentieth in the league. But both teams represented their conferences in the Super Bowl, which seems to suggest that there is something healthy, from an offensive standpoint, about running the ball, even if you're not running it especially well.

So what does this all mean for your team? It means that an elite quarterback and elite receivers do not an offense make. Take the 2014 Tampa Bay Buccaneers, who lacked an elite quarterback—they inexplicably targeted career backup Josh McCown in free agency—but had two high-priced stud receivers in Vincent Jackson and Mike Evans. Both are huge targets and freakish athletes. Both went over 1,000 yards in receiving in 2014, yet Tampa had one of the worst offenses (thirtieth in the league in yards) and teams (2–14) in the NFL. Conversely, in 1990, Stephen Baker led the New York Giants in receiving yards with a modest 540. His team won the Super Bowl. In 1997, Karl Williams led the Tampa Bay Buccaneers with an even more modest 486 receiving yards. His team went 10–6 and advanced to the divisional playoffs.

So it means that while it's sexy to draft wide receivers, perhaps your team would be better off investing its money and draft choices elsewhere. It also means that our Veteran Combine attendees Felix Jones and Michael Bush may find their way back into the league because they (especially Jones) had the ability to get yards per carry (4.7).

And it means that even though we have more money, film, scouting, and resources at our disposal than ever, we're still letting media and perception shape our reality. Since quarterbacks are the league's stars, stars drive television, and the health of television drives how the game is covered, we have this ongoing perception that quarterbacks, receivers, and passing games win titles. While that is undoubtedly good for ratings, it probably isn't the path to victory for your team. Because as the Veteran Combine showed us, it's easier to find an employable back who can rush for four yards per carry than it is to find an elite quarterback.

WEEK THREE: DETROIT AT CONCORD: GREAT FOR A HALF

If football games were only thirty minutes long, I'd be 2–1, as my Lions played a nearly perfect half of football against a far better Concord Colonials squad that featured Hall of Famers in Dave Casper, Steve Largent, and Randy White as well as a certified stud in former Viking linebacker Matt Blair.

Still, it was hard to stay mad for long given the class and good nature of Concord's owner/coach Cela Manka, who was gracious enough to let me bend his ear about sim football.

"Ted, as 'we' enter into older age, nostalgia becomes part of our everyday life. The retro leagues add a certain 'flavor' to remembering the past," he says. Cela is a former insurance man in his sixties and has been playing sim football since I was in diapers. This gives him a unique perspective on the games—as he's coached many thousands of them and called upward of a million plays in competitive games.

"I used to have to drive fifty miles from Pittsburgh to a motel that was already crowded by beer-drinking Steeler fans just to watch the games there because of the fifty-mile 'blackout' policy in those days," he recalls. "Great fun! Loud, happy, contagious—fun. And doubly so if the Steelers actually won!

"My involvement in these sim leagues came about in part by the 'ending of the era' of APBA football board games," he says of the games in which owners would receive mailings with player ratings and lots of math was required to determine a winner. "I played in dozens of those leagues, and I think I am in part responsible for scores of people becoming APBA players. I got my first football and baseball games for Christmas 1964. I saw them advertised on the back of a comic book! We played Foto-Electric football before then. There was a tavern in Garfield that had a huge basement, and a bunch of us would go there and have as many as six to eight games going on at a time. It was the *shit!*

"APBA started to tail off, and I saw an online ad for Action! PC Football. The game *dwarfed* APBA. I started joining leagues, saw the Retros, loved it. Nostalgia is a big thing at my age. I enjoy the sharing with the guys. Most times after a game, we will talk for a while about the game and the past."

One of the most charming things about the Odyssey Football League is the fact that many of the other guys in the league will write up and disseminate little "game stories" via e-mail after they play their weekly matchup. Not all the guys do it, and it's in no way mandatory, but it's one of the sublime little pleasures of retro football, and I find that it helps take the rough edges off losing a game to be able to winsomely write it up.

Below is my write-up of our 42–20 loss to Concord:

> Detroit rolled into Concord with renewed optimism and a 1–1 record thanks largely to the efficient passing of off-season acquisition Bert Jones. The Lions played above themselves and actually took a lead into the halftime locker room, but Concord roared back with a vengeance in the second half, eventually winning 42–20.
>
> Despite consistent double coverage, young Concord signal caller Ron Jaworski repeatedly torched the injury-addled Detroit secondary, finding emerging superstar Steve Largent early and often. Jaworski finished the day with four touchdowns and no interceptions, directing a weapons-laden offense that includes Largent, Wesley Walker, and Dave Casper. Concord's defense kept a lid on

league-leading rookie receiver Wes Chandler, as Jones tossed a pair of scores to Reggie Rucker but also threw up a pair of picks, as he was under siege all day from Colonials linebacker Matt Blair, who picked up three more sacks. As they often are, turnovers were the story of the game, as Lions running back Dexter Bussey continues his penchant for putting the ball on the carpet, losing two more fumbles.

Although Detroit is much improved from a year ago, they are still in need of quality secondary help. Owner/coach Ted Kluck indicated that he would be open to trade talks involving a high-end safety, cornerback, or running back and that first-round picks may be on the table. Never known for his patience, Kluck wants to win now. "I'm pouring myself a scotch and waiting by my rotary-dial telephone," said Kluck of the trade offers he hopes will pour in soon.

Not surprisingly, the trade offers did come and, emboldened by my draft-disdaining research on George Allen, I have started to use my picks as currency with which to purchase existing players. The Concord game, in addition to taking its toll on my ego, also left a mark on my lineup—as I lost safety Tim Gray and defensive tackle Abdul Salaam to injury. I've got depth on the defensive line and will be fine there, but I couldn't afford to lose anyone on my already-mediocre back end.

The owner of the team that I beat in Week Two has been actively shopping half his roster, as he has taken the other approach—building his team through the draft. He's looking for picks in the 1979/1980 drafts while I'm already tired of losing and want to put a competitive team on the field now. He offered to trade me above-average safety Tony Peters (one Pro Bowl in the early 1980s) and cornerback Clarence Chapman, who can provide depth for another few years, as I have two corners retiring following the 1978 season. He originally wanted a second-round pick, which I negotiated down to a third-rounder in 1979. I felt like I added another key piece—a starting-quality safety—without giving much up. Now I have another legitimately good defensive back to pair with the already-good Roger Wehrli. I hope the result will be fewer big plays given up. Hopefully, Largent's torching of me in Week Three will turn out to be the exception rather than the norm, as we successfully shut down Lofton in Week Two.

My season statistics show that I am still struggling to find creative ways to involve the talented David Hill at tight end. He caught an astonishing fifty-three balls in the real 1978 season—more than either of my starting wideouts—and averaged over eleven yards per catch. Thus far, for me, he's caught ten balls through three games but has yet to score. However, if he is taking safety bracket coverage away from Chandler and Rucker, then he is, in a sense, doing his job. By comparison, first-round draft choice and future Hall of Fame tight end Ozzie Newsome has only four catches for thirty-nine yards through three games for another owner. That provides a little perspective on my Hill issues.

7

IN PRAISE OF THE GENTLEMAN FAN

It's been a nightmarish couple of weeks for the global juggernaut known as the National Football League. If you're unaware of what I mean, simply Google the names "Ray Rice" and "Adrian Peterson" (or "Ray McDonald," "Greg Hardy," or "Jonathan Dwyer"). Still, cynic that I am, I wasn't convinced that these scandals would make a real dent in the NFL's ability to do what it does best—get us to part with our money in myriad ways (tickets, jerseys, the NFL Network, fantasy, etc.).

The NFL will survive Ray Rice and Adrian Peterson, but it may not survive its own inflated opinion of itself. I recently purchased the entire library of the NFL Films "season in review" DVDs and Super Bowl highlight films (thank you eBay). I was charmed by how, especially in the 1960s and 1970s, the NFL Films crew treated each season like an experimental art film, using unique angles, filters, and music to tell the story of a season. For all its problems (and there were many problems in the 1960s and 1970s too), football is still a

beautiful, interesting game with no shortage of drama and stories.

There's no denying that we live in a lame era where Twitter
masquerades as journalism and YouTube masquerades as television. Everybody is trying so hard to be funny that nobody is
actually funny anymore. That said, football should be the
thing that is real—real combat between two teams with a
scoreboard at the end telling us who is better. My advice to the
NFL: Give us less. Take away Thursdays. Take away the NFL
Network. Don't expand to eighteen games. Don't make any
more movies. Stop tweeting. Let the game sell itself.

I saw *Draft Day* because I see every football movie whether
it's great (*Jerry Maguire*) or terrible (*Leatherheads*, which I'm
ashamed of owning and watching multiple times, waiting for it
to be good) or could have been great but was actually mediocre (*Any Given Sunday*, which I also own all sixteen hours of)
or is quantifiably terrible but is still a great piece of craptastic
1990s nostalgia that I've viewed a shameful number of times
(*The Program*).

This is actually a commentary on the commentary about
Draft Day. Today, nearly every sports media outlet on the
planet now employs a "columnist" who once spent some time
working as an NFL scout. They do this because this supposedly gives credibility to the columnist's opinion about all things
NFL related. This has resulted in a ton of the following in the
wake of the release of *Draft Day*: "According to former NFL
scout [Name] of Fox Sports Altoona, *Draft Day* is unrealis-
tic."

For the most part, the movies I mentioned above proliferat-
ed before the Internet/social media age and before the every-

columnist-is-a-former-(whatever)-making-him-an-expert-on-(whatever) phenomenon, before "breaking a story" meant going on Twitter and saying something. What I mean is that it was better when we didn't have a bunch of former sports agents online ripping the veracity of *Jerry Maguire* or a bunch of NFL-player-turned-columnists around to eviscerate *Any Given Sunday*, which, admittedly, was evisceratable on many ridiculous levels (e.g., eyeballs rolling down the field and Willie Beamen reading the paper on the sidelines while eating a concession stand hot dog). These movies had some room to breathe and be universally enjoyed because there weren't a bunch of experts online yet telling us to think that the movies were actually stupid and making us feel stupid for liking them. And even though *Leatherheads* was released in the Internet age, there were no 1920s-era football players around to rip it. (According to 120-year-old former Canton Bulldog Frankie Conzelman, *Leatherheads* is a joke.)

Candor: I don't like the current state of sports media. Saying this makes me sound like an old person, which I sort of am. I long for the old days when a given columnist may not have known what he was talking about but wrote well as opposed to today, when there are way too many people writing, many of whom are experts in whatever they're talking about but most of whom don't care about a beautiful sentence or whatever. I miss walking to the mailbox as a kid on Friday afternoons and getting my issue of *Sports Illustrated* and immediately flipping to the back page to read whatever Rick Reilly wrote because of how well it was written.

Draft Day was panned as semi-stupid before people even got a chance to enjoy it in spite of the campiness that was there because the movie was signed off on by the NFL itself, almost guaranteeing that it wouldn't say anything important. But ironically, in Oliver Stone's relentless pursuit of saying something important, *Any Given Sunday* actually ended up still being pretty stupid and campy but still enjoyable, which is the point of a movie.

And this, in fact, is the point of the NFL. However, in our quest to be clever, I think we've lost this simple truth. Mine is the generation that fully and irrevocably embraced irony as religion because being too clever for something meant that that something could never hurt us. For example, if we never allow ourselves to be fully charmed by the NFL again and our defense mechanism against this is a sort of sneering cleverer-than-thou online posture, then the NFL can never disappoint us.

Wrote David Foster Wallace in his postmodern epic *Infinite Jest*, "This is because irony, entertaining as it is, serves an almost exclusively negative function. It's critical and destructive, a ground-clearing. . . . Irony's singularly unuseful when it comes to constructing anything to replace the hypocrisies it debunks."[1]

Irony, wrote Wallace, should have only "emergency use." However, we have made it the backbone of nearly every piece of current sportswriting and fan-response comment circulating and constantly updated online. "What really upset him," wrote Wallace biographer D. T. Max, "was when Burger King used irony to sell hamburgers, or Joe Isuzu, cars."[2]

"The Baby Boomers lived through American institutions' loss of credibility, but it was their Gen-X children who grew up inhaling skepticism and exhaling cynicism," explains historian Cory Hartman. "Time will tell if the Millennials believe again or if they press the doubt to new depths."

Irony, in a sports sense, could be defended as a natural pendulum swing away from the "all professional athletes are great guys and role models" ethos of the 1950s. But I think the point has been made in full. We know that athletes are human and fallible. I myself have abused irony in print and indeed used it to start making a writing career in the early 2000s, writing snarky little bits of satire for *ESPN the Magazine.* Similar to Wallace, I think I have had moments of real conviction on this matter and have been trying for some time to cultivate the courage to just write what I mean. For me, participation in the sim league, with the random collection of older owners and football enthusiasts, is a step away from irony and a step toward loving the game again.

In the early 1990s, David Foster Wallace wrote snarkily but lovingly about the Illinois State Fair for *Harper's* magazine. In the essay, he both pillories the fairgoer's obsession with entertainment-as-filler-of-void but also indicts himself and highlights those things that were truly laudable. However, his concern was that, according to biographer D. T. Max, "the people were gluttons and the animals miserable."[3]

I fear the same for us as modern-day football fans. I fear that our appetite for the game is gluttonous but that we—and the players—are rendered more and more miserable by it. I fear that there's a day-after-day joylessness in the drone of the NFL Network and the never-ending noise of the online comment section. I fear that, for its omnipresence, the game has been rendered that much less special.

Today, sports talk radio and social media are ablaze with a debate as to whether Dallas Cowboys wide receiver Dez Bryant did or didn't hit his mother with a baseball cap in a

Wal-Mart parking lot. You can't make this stuff up. This is what NFL fandom has come to. As of now, it's a story about a rumor about an alleged video of an alleged incident. And, of course, nary a week can go by without commentators on social media calling for everyone involved in the incident—from Dez Bryant to *Pro Football Talk*'s Mike Florio—to be fired.

"The other reason that anti-institutionalism pertains to sports is that individual sports figures are mini-institutions like never before," explains Hartman. "The phenomenon itself is going on a century old (thank you, Babe Ruth). But today's media, standard and social, has the suppleness, resources, penetration, and ubiquity to ignite a galaxy of stars for fans and voyeurs to consume more or less continuously and at will."

For me, it just underscores what I love so much about retro football and the sim league: the fact that there are no rumors, stories, TMZ videos, or tweets circulating about the players that we're enjoying from 1978. In a sense, to us, they are nothing more than their statistics, but in another very real way, it serves to further *humanize* them in a way that Dez Bryant and Adrian Peterson can't be human right now. Bryant and Peterson *are* their stories. They are a human pastiche of every ugly headline, photo, tweet, grainy cell phone video, or sports talk show caller, and they will be as such until the balm of years and decades can smooth away those rough edges. Brian Sipe and Dexter Bussey—thanks to the intervening thirty-five years that have elapsed since their moments in the spotlight—have gone back to just being human. There are no stories circulating about them and their vices, which no doubt exist but are dealt with privately.

That is not to say that there aren't painful stories as we sift through the names that populated the league in 1978. The future Pro Bowl safety for whom I recently traded, Tony Peters, was involved in the NFL's late 1970s to early 1980s cocaine boom, which included other sim-league standouts, like Chuck Muncie, Pete Johnson, Ross Browner, and Scott Studwell. Peters was arrested in his dormitory room during training camp in the summer of 1983 on cocaine charges, including conspiracy to distribute, and was suspended by the Redskins. He pleaded guilty and received a four-year suspended sentence. He was suspended by the league for the 1983 season. In January 1981, star Dallas Cowboys linebacker Thomas "Hollywood" Henderson admitted to a $1,200-per-day cocaine habit.[4] So, far be it from me to suggest that there is something purer about a bygone era. There isn't. There was sin, deceit, and human depravity in 1978 just as there is now. However, today, there is a loud and constant barrage of it via social media such that we are privy to the worst of people—celebrity or otherwise—all the time. And not only are we privy, but we are invited to participate.

Take the case of former Nebraska Cornhusker Johnny "The Jet" Rodgers. He was voted Nebraska's "Player of the Century" and won the 1972 Heisman Trophy as an all-around rushing, receiving, and kick-returning threat in the days before specialization rendered triple-threat players largely obsolete. Rodgers was the star of what is considered college football's "Game of the Century"—a game in which he returned a punt seventy-two yards to score Nebraska's first touchdown in a 35–31 victory over Oklahoma.

But by 1978, Rodgers had reached the end of a strange professional career that started with the CFL's Montreal Alouettes after he spurned the NFL for a more lucrative contract in Canada. Rodgers played four distinguished years in the CFL before ending his career with two injury-marred and disappointing seasons with the San Diego Chargers.

Rodgers's personal struggles were chronicled in detail in Armen Keteyian's *Big Red Confidential*, in which he describes in detail a trial ending in a gun charge conviction for Rodgers. He writes, "Another attorney ended up keeping Rodgers's Heisman Trophy in lieu of an unpaid legal tab. In February 1987 that trophy sat on the defense table before Superior Court judge Jack Levitt, who stared out at Rodgers and the rest of the courtroom. Rodgers had finally defended himself at a jury trial and lost. . . . At sentencing time Levitt looked first at the trophy and then at Rodgers before he addressed Rodgers and the courtroom. 'You've ridden that horse far too long,' he said. 'Mr. Rodgers expects to be treated differently. As a society maybe we're somewhat to blame. We give respect and adulation to athletes and then all of a sudden there is a big fall, and they're treated like everyone else.'"[5]

It is surreal, though, in the sim league to be dealing in players who are disabled or dead to some degree *because* of the game they played so well, which we celebrate and are nostalgic for.

"In 2009 without my even realizing it, life changed," wrote legendary running back (and 1978 first-round draft choice) Earl Campbell in a *Yahoo! Sports* piece. "I was recovering from my fifth back operation after having been diagnosed with a genetic condition called spinal stenosis, in which my spinal cord canal became so narrow that it compressed my nerves. To dull the unbearable and constant pain, my doctor prescribed me high potency pain medication in the form of Vicodin and Oxycontin. Without my doctor's knowledge and without even thinking it was a problem, I began washing my pain pills down with Budweiser. Quickly I began spiraling out of control."[6]

Campbell was a Heisman Trophy winner, an NFL All-Pro, and now a Pro Football Hall of Famer, but his vicious running style, combined with the league's AstroTurf era, has made it hard to walk without the use of a walker. "I did something to my body to get that, and you know what I did," said Campbell in an Associated Press report in 2012. "I think some of it came from playing football, playing the way I did."[7]

The story of former Tampa Bay Bucs running back Jerry Eckwood is less well known but is sad in a similar way. Eckwood was an important cog in the 1979 worst-to-first Buc squad quarterbacked by Doug Williams, who was another 1978 draft choice. According to a 2010 *Tampa Tribune* piece, Eckwood was living in a long-term care facility as a result of concussions he sustained as a player at Arkansas and then later as a Tampa Bay Buc. Eckwood, a punishing runner and lead blocker, was the true unknown soldier. When asked how many concussions he sustained, he couldn't remember and simply replied, "A lot . . . a lot."

"When Jerry played with us, he would walk to the wrong huddle sometimes," remembered Gay Culverhouse in the piece. Her father, Hugh Culverhouse, owned the Buccaneers at the time. "Players would have to get him and steer him back to the Bucs. Or sometimes he would walk to the opposing bench when it was time to come off the field."

This begs the obvious questions: Where was the team doctor? Where were the trainers? If the owner's daughter noticed Eckwood's compromised mental state, why didn't everybody else?

Eckwood played for only three seasons, never made a Pro Bowl, never rushed for over 1,000 yards in a season, and never averaged over four yards per carry. Even more chilling about his story is the fact that he didn't play for a decade. He did maximum damage to his body over a relatively short period of time. In the piece, he recalls "being knocked out on the field after hits from opponents Clay Matthews, Doug Plank, and Gary Fencik." All of those names are key players in our 1978 sim league. All of them took something real and tangible out of Jerry Eckwood—not out of malice or hatred but because it was what the game required.[8]

Playing and enjoying sim football is, for me, a way of honoring the Jerry Eckwoods. It's a way to enjoy their mastery of their jobs and honor their achievements because whereas fantasy football is concerned with a few superstars and the here/now/future, sim football requires a knowledge of the Jerry Eckwoods of the league—roster players who grind hard to stay in the game and make a living in professional football. Our rosters are full of such players—names like Mark Arneson, Brad Oates, Don Hardeman, and Barry Bennett.

"People living painfully humdrum-yet-complicated lives seek purity in sports," says Hartman. "Sports promise purity in all kinds of ways, from the crisp line at the boundary of the field or court, to the uniform (ponder the word: *uni-form*), to the cut-and-dried arithmetic of scoreboard and standings, and to the nostalgic, resonant echoes of younger, simpler days. Even as we are drawn magnetically toward sports, however, we do not forget that institutions are peddling these wares— the wares *are* institutions—and institutions are never to be trusted. Institutions will always betray us."

Sim football is a move away from the institution of pro football and a move toward honoring the individuals who played it. What I appreciate most is the fact that there is no inflammatory language used when discussing players. Perhaps it's the age of my co-owners, but there are no online exchanges about players who "suck" or "are useless." That kind of language is replaced with nostalgia and appreciation.

It's not a wide-eyed and childish appreciation, but it's the kind of appreciation that chooses to overlook flaws and enjoy what there is to enjoy. In that, it's not unlike a long marriage where the spouses are no longer convinced of each other's perfection but rather choose to overlook each other's many flaws in a way that serves to deepen the bond.

WEEK FOUR: MONTREAL AT DETROIT: SNOW-BLIND

Montreal 17, Detroit 16

There are some who say that Detroit is the most depressing place on earth, and today certainly bore that out—starting with a game played in an inexplicable snowstorm inside the Pontiac Silverdome. "It must have been a microclimate," said Lions coach Ted Kluck, who knows nothing about science. He also, at times, appears to know nothing about scoring points on a football field.

Detroit outgained Montreal 413 yards to 192, largely on the legs of Dexter Bussey and Kevin Long. But the woes continued for Detroit, as Bert Jones was carted off the snow-covered Silverdome floor with an injury that will keep him out for ten weeks. Jones's understudy Brian Sipe had an efficient day in relief going 8–10 for 111 yards and a scoring strike to his favorite target of a year ago, Reggie

Rucker. "There is reason for optimism," said Kluck, who admittedly didn't look or feel optimistic while shuffling off the field through the snow.

"Vince and the Alouettes played a great game," he said. "And I got a great second half of coaching from my assistant Tristan Kluck," who took the reins from his father while the former was treating frostbite.

As has been their custom, key mistakes doomed Detroit. The Lions gave up a seventy-three-yard punt return for a score to Jackie Wallace, and Lions kicker Frank Corral shanked an extra point that would have sent the game into overtime. Corral, who came to the Lions via Los Angeles, expressed that kicking in an indoor snowstorm was "disconcerting." The Lions also had a punt block, as the menagerie of "things that can go wrong on a football field" continued. And while Detroit successfully shut down Alouettes playmaker Haven Moses (zero catches), they had no answer for rejuvenated defensive end Jack Gregory, who had a career day, collecting nine tackles and two sacks. "Jack Gregory was a revelation," said Kluck. "Why couldn't he have done that for us last year?"

What I know about Week Four is that I lost the game by one point—a point that would have been either there or inconsequential had any of the following happened:

1. Frank Corrall hit a chip-shot extra point following a game-tying touchdown catch by Reggie Rucker in the fourth quarter.
2. We hadn't given up a punt return for a touchdown, which, in real life, happens for a reason, but in sim-computer life is simply a function of randomness and chance.

3. We also hadn't had a punt blocked, leading to a Montreal field goal (see above regarding randomness and chance).

What I also know is that we were ten-point underdogs per the computer line but lost by only a point. I also know that we finally got our running game rolling in a consistent way, with Bussey, Long, and even my blocking back Hardeman all putting up big numbers. Rucker and Chandler, after slow starts against Montreal, again proved to be very effective. David Hill had a couple of key drive-sustaining catches for me. However, the fact remains that we're 1–3, and I'm feeling what many real-life NFL general managers and coaches must feel when they look at the talent they've compiled versus the reality of their record: panic. Instead of doing what I should do, which is staying the course, I am still looking for quick fixes—for trades that will stave off the losing feeling.

Still, I know in my heart that we should have beaten Montreal. We held the league's third-leading receiver—Haven Moses—to zero catches. He didn't have a back over a hundred yards, and his quarterback Mike Livingston—who torched me last year—did nothing. But again, turnover differential and big plays tell the story. He had two takeaways (a fumble and a pick), three counting the blocked punt. I had zero. This was the story of the game.

Losing Bert Jones hurts but isn't surprising, as I knew he'd be healthy for only a few games in 1978. And Sipe played well in relief. But I'm getting some trade offers for Sipe (nothing good yet), but perhaps I can sell him off to regain some of the picks I've already dealt or for a marquee player who can help my struggling defense.

8

IT'S AN ANSWER

The Ballad of the Big Back

One immutable law of the football universe is that if my team runs for 3.5 yards on three plays in a row, we get to keep the football, and we get a fresh set of downs. This principle can be used to cover mediocre quarterbacking (e.g., the Parcells-era Giants, especially in the O. J. Anderson years), and it can also be used to hide a complete lack of talent at the wide receiver position (e.g., the 1999 Tennessee Titans, the Eddie George era).

But as spread offenses proliferate, especially at the college level, big backs are at risk of becoming an extinct species. I think this is a mistake. Below I'll break down a list of some of the NFL's leading rushers over the last decade and a half and look for some patterns both in their physical stature and in the makeup of their backfields:

> Adrian Peterson–Jerome Felton: Peterson is a sturdy 6'2″
>   and 215, and he put up crazy post-ACL numbers in 2012
>   behind the blocking of old-school jackhammer Jerome

Felton (6'0" and 246, fifth-round draft choice). The Peterson–Felton combination kept Minnesota competitive and masked a serious lack of talent at quarterback (Christian Ponder) and, Harvin excluded, the same at wide receiver, where the Vikings rolled out a who's who of NFL journeymen and disappointments.

Ray Rice–Vonta Leach: Although he doesn't fit my size profile (more later), Rice has posted four straight 1,000-yard seasons dating back to 2009. He has done so behind the best fullback in the league—Vonta Leach (6'0" and 246, undrafted in 2004).

Arian Foster–Vonta Leach: An undrafted free agent himself, Foster fits the size profile (6'0" and 232) and put up a ridiculous 1,600-yard season in 2010 behind, you guessed it, Vonta Leach. Foster has the size to finish runs and the vision to find what's blocked for him, and he's made Matt Schaub look better than he actually is.

Jamal Lewis–Alan Ricard: Before Ray Rice and Vonta Leach, there was Lewis (5'11" and 241) and Ricard (5'11" and 237, undrafted out of Louisiana–Monroe). Semi-quietly, Lewis put up seven 1,000-plus-yard seasons and averaged 4.2 yards per carry for his career. He was the ultimate hammer on a bad Baltimore offense that won a Super Bowl with Trent Dilfer under center (i.e., minimizing the quarterback position).

Eddie George–Lorenzo Neal: Eddie George was a punishing 6'3" and 240, and while he didn't have a real long career, when he was good, he was very good and could consistently generate pile-moving, 3.5-yard carries to power a Titan offense whose only other star was tight end Frank Wycheck. George had his best statistical years running behind his era's rock-star fullback, Lorenzo Neal (5'11" and 255, fourth-round draft pick). Neal was a punishing isolation blocker who eliminated opposing linebackers for George and, later, LaDainian Tomlinson and Lorenzo Neal.

LaDainian Tomlinson–Lorenzo Neal: LaDainian Tomlinson had the luxury of spending most of his brilliant Hall of Fame career running behind Neal, who was the Rolls-Royce of NFL fullbacks, before passing that torch to Vonta Leach.

What do LaDainian Tomlinson, Eddie George, Ray Rice, and Arian Foster all have in common? They've all run behind elite fullbacks Lorenzo Neal or Vonta Leach at some point in their careers, and they've done so in offenses with limited talent at quarterback. So perhaps NFL teams, instead of looking for the next boom-or-bust wide receiver, should be looking for the next isolation beast at fullback. My reasoning? As offenses spread out, defenses will become smaller and faster, making them susceptible to the kind of straight-ahead isolation blocking that will benefit a backfield with nearly 500 pounds of combined bulk. Since I believe it's easier to find a good fullback and a good, big tailback than it is to find an elite passer, the pendulum will and should swing back to big backfields eventually. The logic here is that it's easier to figure out how to get 3.5 yards per play, and there's less risk in that than there is in throwing the ball down the field and all over the field. In the words of the immortal Rod Tidwell, "It ain't sexy, but it's an answer."

That said, I made a list before the 2013 draft of players who were undervalued and overvalued based on the model above.

Undervalued big backs who can generate yards and move chains are the following:

LeVeon Bell, Michigan State: Bell is 6′2″ and 245 and had more yards after contact than anyone in college football last year. He has experience running behind a fullback, and if I were drafting a running back this year, he'd be my first off the board. Bell was his team's entire offense in 2012.

Knile Davis, Arkansas: Davis is 6′0″ and 226 and blazed a 4.37-second forty-yard dash at the NFL Scouting Combine. Along with the rest of the Razorbacks, he was a victim of the gong show that was Arkansas football over the past twelve months. He was also in a crowded backfield with . . .

Ronnie Wingo Jr., Arkansas: Wingo is 6′2″ and 231 and ran a 4.47-second forty-yard dash at his Pro Day, so he fits the height/weight/speed profile we're looking for in a modern-day big back.

Zach Line, SMU: Line is 6′0″ and 232 and Caucasian, which is why he gets misrepresented as (and will most likely gain fifteen pounds and end up becoming) a fullback. Line ran for over 4,100 yards in his career at SMU, adding forty-seven rushing touchdowns. Like Mike Alstott before him, he has "feature back" tools.

Overvalued backs include the following:

Giovani Bernard, North Carolina: Only 5′9″ and 210 with an injury history and questionable pass protection.

Jonathan Franklin, UCLA: 5′10″ and 201, with a thin upper and lower body.

Marcus Lattimore, South Carolina: By all accounts, a great
kid with a great story but should have been ranked behind LeVeon Bell regardless of the injury. Average
speed.

Andre Ellington, Clemson: 5'9" and 197. Meh.

I was right on LeVeon Bell (in a big way) and to a certain
extent Knile Davis, who has shown promise in Kansas City. I
was initially wrong about Gio Bernard (who was a big contributor as a rookie in Cincinnati) and Ellington, who did some
nice things for Arizona in his rookie campaign. But both guys
are averaging less than four yards per carry and will fall far
short of 1,000 yards in 2014. Franklin has done nothing, and
Lattimore is out of football.

Meanwhile, Jeremy Hill (6'0" and 233, averaging 5.0 yards
per carry) and LeVeon Bell (1,348 rushing yards, 4.8 yards per
carry) are near the top of the league in rushing. Both weigh
over 230 pounds, and both carry the mantle of primary ballcarrier for their club. Hill ended the season as one of 2014's top
rookies at any position.

2015 PROSPECTS

Based on the above criteria, I've targeted the following running back prospects for next-level success. All of the backs
below fit my size profile, and all have worked from pro-style
offenses in college, which serves to further prepare them for
what they'll encounter at the next level:

Todd Gurley, 6'1 " and 232, Georgia: Todd Gurley is this
draft's highest-rated running back prospect but also
something of an enigma, being that he tore an ACL in

2014 and missed half the season. Still, he has a rare
blend of speed and power and in 2014 gained an amazing 61.9 percent of his yards *after* making contact with a
defender. Gurley is aggressive and finishes runs with
physicality. I studied Gurley's Clemson film, which was
his best statistical outing in 2014—a year in which he
averaged an astonishing 7.4 yards per carry. I saw a back
who runs effectively behind a fullback and craves contact. Of all the big backs to follow on this list, Gurley is
the one who really runs like a nasty, physical, big back.
He makes defenders feel all of his 232 pounds. Gurley
showed game-breaking speed on the Clemson tape, taking a kickoff return to the house. Gurley showed the
ability to make one critical cut and get upfield on routine
run plays. He gets everything he can out of each run and
moves the pile. This is a special prospect.

Javorius "Buck" Allen, 6'0" and 221, USC: Allen ran a
serviceable 4.53-second forty-yard dash at the NFL
Scouting Combine. I broke down his 2014 Cal tape and
saw a player who is a smooth, patient, one-cut back with
the ability to catch the ball out of the backfield. Allen
found the sledding tough for much of the Cal game (it
was one of his worst statistically) but was still a vital
part of his team's offense, picking up some key first
downs both on the ground and through the air. Allen was
a true dual threat in his USC career, racking up over
2,300 yards on the ground with a 5.5-yards-per-carry
average and catching an additional sixty-three passes for
710 yards and two scores as a receiver. He's not quite as
physical as I'd like him to be given his size, but he has

the bulk and skill set to be a punishing three-down back at the next level.

T. J. Yeldon, 6′1″ and 226, Alabama: Like a number of Alabama backs before him, T. J. Yeldon chose to turn pro early because he was losing carries to a younger player. Yeldon is a little bit of an enigma in that he was highly heralded at Alabama but ran a pedestrian forty-yard dash (4.61) at the NFL Scouting Combine and seemed to phase out of the offense a little bit in 2014. Still, he finished his career at Alabama with over 3,300 yards with an impressive 5.8-yards-per-carry average. I studied Yeldon's Auburn tape from 2014, which was his most impressive statistical outing of the season. Alabama was under the influence of offensive coordinator Lane Kiffin in 2014 and, as such, ran more shotgun/spread-type plays than in years past. One of Yeldon's most intriguing characteristics, to me, is his vision and patience. He sees things develop and can move laterally in the hole. He also runs well behind a fullback on Alabama's power plays and shows a nose for the end zone in short yardage. Yeldon can set his feet and stone blitzers in pass protection but more often simply throws a shoulder at them.

David Johnson, 6′1″ and 224, Northern Iowa: Johnson is a small-school prospect who saw many of his carries come from the pistol formation in 2014. Still, many of those carries were on pretty standard NFL-type run plays behind a less-than-spectacular offensive line. I studied Johnson's 2014 Illinois State tape and found a player who, like Allen, looked smooth and athletic out of the backfield and, when he ran to the hole with aggressiveness, gained positive yardage. But, like Allen, he sometimes plays smaller than his 224 pounds. He's a little eager to cut plays to the backside but can have a nasty burst when he wants to. Like Allen, he averaged 5.4 yards per carry for his college career (three seasons over 1,000 yards) and caught an impressive 141 balls for over 1,700 yards. Johnson had over 200 yards receiving against Big Ten foe Iowa. Johnson can provide value in the return game as well and took a kick to the house in the Illinois State film. He did it all for Northern Iowa.

Aaron Ripkowski, 6'1" and 257, fullback, Oklahoma: Ripkowski is a big, athletic, old-school isolation lead blocker in the mold of a Lorenzo Neal or Vonta Leach. Ripkowski successfully lead blocked for a variety of impressive Oklahoma running backs, most recently the record-breaking Samaje Perine. Ripkowski will be a late-round pick who will go largely unnoticed by most NFL fans but will provide real value as a lead blocker in traditional schemes that incorporate a fullback.

THE CHICAGO BEARS: A CASE STUDY

If there were ever a team that has the personnel makeup for an overhaul of the type I'm proposing above, it's the Chicago Bears. Let's look at what the Bears have:

1. A bad quarterback: Say what you want about Jay Cutler (and many people have), I just don't see "savior" and "franchise" production out of him. His statistical production of late has been on par with the likes of Carson Palmer and Ryan Fitzpatrick, and he fell short of the top

ten in every meaningful statistical category last season. Unless Marc Trestman works a miracle with Cutler, what the Bears have is a great candidate to be "hidden" by other players in the offense. I believe they need to take the ball out of Cutler's hands in a significant way and play to their strengths as a club. Cutler needs to be viewed less as Tony Romo and more like Trent Dilfer.

2. Two capable big backs.[1] Matt Forte fits the size profile at 6'1" and 221 and has three 1,000-yard seasons under his belt. However, he appears to be at something of a crossroads, as the Bears have never been able to figure out who they are offensively and quite how they want to use Forte. The Bears also acquired Michael Bush, who at 6'2" and 243 fits the size profile and has averaged over four yards per carry for his career.

3. An offensive line that can't pass protect: The only statistical category in which Cutler cracked the top ten was times sacked (fifth) and sack yards lost (fourth). Granted, not all of this is on the offensive line. Some of it is on Cutler himself—a phenomenon (taking sacks) that has less to do with athleticism (Cutler is fast and athletic) and more to do with an innate "inner clock," or sense for when and how to get rid of the football.

The Bears have never consistently passed the football. Blame it on Soldier Field, the cold weather, or the wind off of Lake Michigan, but for whatever reason, they've never passed the ball with any modicum of consistency. And while they finally have some talent at wide receiver (Brandon Marshall and Alshon Jeffery), they would be wise to utilize the big-back resources at their disposal.

THE CURIOUS CASE OF TRENT RICHARDSON (AND THE DEATH OF THE FEATURE BACK)

Indianapolis Colts running back Trent Richardson was drafted third overall by the Cleveland Browns behind Andrew Luck and Robert Griffin III in the 2012 NFL Draft. He started all but one game as a rookie and failed to reach 1,000 yards in what was statistically his best season. In 2013, he was traded to the Indianapolis Colts, who are, it seems, forever in need of a running game. On paper, everything about Richardson makes sense: he has good size (228 pounds) and played for Nick Saban in a pro-style college offense where he was both a hammer and a human highlight reel.

In real life, he has been a disappointment. He averaged an anemic three yards per carry in 2013 and currently has 475 yards and a 3.3-yards-per-carry average as the 2014 season winds down. He has not provided an answer to Indy's needs at running back, and, in fact, Daniel "Boom" Herron, a former sixth-round pick and a practice squad acquisition from the Bengals, has given the Colts the backfield upgrade they thought they'd get with Richardson. Herron runs angrier and more decisively and is averaging 5.1 yards per carry since he began vulturing touches from Richardson in Week Twelve of the 2014 season.

The Colts have tried seemingly everything imaginable to try to jump-start Richardson. They've run him behind a full-back in a conventional I formation, they've run him with double tight ends in a single-back set, and they've run him out of the spread. Nothing has worked. Looking at the coaches' film from Week Six at Houston, their approach seemed to be "put

Richardson behind a fullback and run him." It didn't work. Later in the season, against Washington in Week Thirteen, the approach was "run Richardson from the spread." It was even less successful.

What the Colts haven't done, really since Edgerrin James, is commit to a single back and commit to the running game in general. This season, through fourteen weeks, they're running the ball 37.05 percent of the time, ranking twenty-eighth in the league. In 2013, they ran the ball only 38 percent of the time. Seattle, Super Bowl champions after the 2013 season, has led the league in percentage of run plays each of the last three seasons—running the ball well over half the time, which is kind of astonishing in today's NFL. They've done it largely behind a classic and traditional "feature back" in Marshawn Lynch (5'11" and 215). And what's readily apparent is that the Seahawks have invested heavily in their offensive line:

Offensive tackle Russell Okung, sixth-overall pick, 2006
Offensive guard James Carpenter, twenty-fifth-overall
   pick, 2011
Offensive guard Max Unger, C, second-round pick, 2009
Offensive guard J. R. Sweezy, seventh-round pick, 2012—
   a converted defensive tackle out of North Carolina State
Right tackles Breno Giacommini and Michael Bowie (both
   players are unremarkable, both were late-round picks
   [fifth and seventh, respectively], and neither player is
   with Seattle in 2014)

By contrast, the Indianapolis offensive line in 2013 featured the following:

Offensive tackle Anthony Castonzo, twenty-second pick,
   2011

Offensive guard Donald Thomas, sixth round, 2008 (via the
    Miami Dolphins)

Offensive guard Hugh Thornton, third round, 2013

Offensive guard Mike McGlynn, fourth round, 2008 (via
    the Philadelphia Eagles—the Colts were his third team,
    and he's on number four now)

Center Samson Satele, second round, 2007 (via the Miami
    Dolphins—the Colts are his third team)

Offensive tackle Gosder Cherilus, seventeenth-overall pick,
    2007 (via the Detroit Lions)

What's apparent after looking at both lineups is that, with the
exception of the right tackle position, Seattle invested heavily
and often in its own players, and for the most part, those
players have worked out. The Colts, by contrast, started two
ex-Dolphins, an ex-Eagle, and an ex-Lion. Cherilus was a bust
in Detroit, McGlynn is a journeyman who continues to journey, and Thomas was underwhelming in Miami. Castonzo has
been solid if unspectacular as a Colt thus far.

Looking closer at both rosters, it's clear that Seattle chose
to surround 2012 draft pick Russell Wilson (quarterback) with
offensive linemen and a running game, while the Colts chose
to surround their franchise quarterback Andrew Luck (also
2012) with wide receivers and pricey tight ends. The Colts
have their currency tied up in tight ends Coby Fleener and
Dwayne Allen and wide receivers T. Y. Hilton, Reggie
Wayne, and Hakeem Nicks. Hence, they have one of the worst
rush offenses in the league.

CONVENTIONAL DRAFT WISDOM AND
THE RUNNING BACK

The conventional draft myth is that running backs with too many college carries will break down early in the NFL. This is just flat wrong, yet it is the reason why each year there are players with tantalizing height/weight/speed combinations who are overdrafted based on "potential" and "upside." In a nutshell, I would rather have the player who was trusted by his college coach to get yards and win games. Two examples of players who had *truckloads* of college carries but went on to long, productive NFL careers are Emmitt Smith (700 college carries in the SEC) and Barry Sanders (523 college carries). By contrast, players in the same era, like Sammie Smith (411), Tim Worley (364), and Jarrod Bunch (311), had relatively few college carries and tantalizing height/weight/speed profiles. All flopped at the pro level.

Some modern-day examples of seemingly "overworked" college backs who had productive pro careers include Larry Johnson (460 college carries) and LaDainian Tomlinson, who had a jaw-dropping 943 college carries and will soon be in the Hall of Fame. The point: there are guys each draft who are going to get screwed for being *too* productive in college. This is a shame.

Wisconsin's Montee Ball will get dinged for his excessive college carries (924), but he had an ultra-productive career getting yards in a pro-style offense in a competitive conference. Ditto for Nebraska's Rex Burkhead and Vanderbilt's Zac Stacy—two ultra-productive players who were day three bargains and will be productive NFL players.

PERCEPTION AND REALITY AT THE RUNNING BACK POSITION

I recently had lunch with a friend who, for a time, shared my obsession with all things NFL Draft related. For us, this basically manifested itself in buying lots of magazines and thinking we were going to "revolutionize" the draft process by somehow figuring out something that everybody else somehow wasn't figuring out—meaning that we wanted to be *Moneyball* for the NFL Draft, which made us not unlike everyone else like that.

Anyway, we had lunch, and part of the lunch involved him bringing his huge stack of draft magazines for us to comb through—again, ostensibly for some kind of higher intellectual purpose but really just for fun. I settled on ESPN's inaugural draft guide, which featured Reggie Bush on the cover and has—in the years since 2006—undergone a life cycle that includes "breathless, excited magazine launch!" to "people are getting all of this on the Internet but still for some reason buying draft magazines" to "people are getting all of this on the Internet and have finally stopped buying draft magazines" (now).

The 2006 NFL Draft is an interesting study in how nobody knows anything. This is going to sound like I'm picking on the Scouts, Inc., "experts" at ESPN, but their experts are no different than the "experts" at *The Sporting News* or even, at some level, the actual experts picking the actual players. Here are some examples:

1. They had fifteen wide receivers rated ahead of Greg Jennings (on whom they had a fourth-round grade), none

of whom (besides Santonio Holmes) have done anything especially noteworthy in the NFL. Some names include Chad Jackson, Derek Hagan, Travis Wilson, and everyone's favorite "sleeper" that year, Hank Baskett. What's interesting about scouting is that it's supposed to be the art of finding guys who can play and, as such, determining which guys can't play at the NFL level. It's not, theoretically, the art of slotting people into rounds on a draft board. What I'm trying to say is that if there was really only one or two receivers on the entire board who could play in the NFL in 2006, they should have had only one or two ranked. The same thing happened in ESPN's 2007 draft magazine at the quarterback position. The cover of the magazine featured an image of Brady Quinn with the words "Brady Quinn Can't Fail." He did, of course, fail and is now out of football, as is first-overall pick JaMarcus Russell, on whom the hapless Raiders staked their quarterbacking hopes. ESPN Scouts, Inc., ranked twenty-five quarterbacks in 2007, and really only two of them—Kevin Kolb and Matt Moore—did anything of note in the NFL. Matt Moore was an undrafted free agent and thus far has started twenty-five NFL games, completed nearly 60 percent of his passes, and has a touchdown-to-interception ratio of thirty-three to twenty-eight, which begs the question: is anybody in the industry (scouts or even media "scouts") willing to say, in effect, there are no quarterbacks in this year's class who can play?

2. Their top-rated quarterback was Matt Leinart, which is an honest mistake because a lot of people (including the Arizona Cardinals and me) missed on Matt Leinart in

2006. More interesting is the rest of the quarterback class. They had a second-round grade on Omar Jacobs, who never made an NFL roster, and third-round grades on Darrell Hackney and Charlie Whitehurst. Arguably the best quarterback in the 2006 class not named "Jay Cutler" was Toledo's Bruce Gradkowski, who has given quality snaps as a spot starter to the Bengals and the Raiders and who is the kind of guy who is always in the process of being replaced but who is usually always better than the guy doing the replacing. They had a fifth-round grade on Gradkowski behind such stalwarts as Reggie McNeal and Paul Pinegar. With the exception of Cutler and Gradkowski, none of the ESPN-rated quarterbacks in the 2006 class have done anything of note.

3. You could argue that tight end was the "filet" of the 2006 draft, featuring names like Owen Daniels and Vernon Davis and lesser-but-still-productive names like Marcedes Lewis, Anthony Fasano, and Tony Scheffler. To their credit, ESPN got most of these right. They were also strong on defensive ends, giving somewhat high grades to guys like Elvis Dumervil and Tamba Hali, but they got mostly slaughtered in the secondary (Darnell Bing in the first round anyone?). Incidentally, the same could be said the following year, when they wrote of "all-world" corner Darrelle Revis, "Lacks elite speed and quick-twitch athleticism. Substandard lateral quickness. Will struggle to match up with some NFL receivers one-on-one. Doesn't show much acceleration on returns." Umm, okay. Today, Revis is the consensus best cover guy in the league, just won a Super Bowl ring in

New England, and just became the richest defensive back in pro football in free agency.

4. An example of ridiculousness in the "scouting reports" that come in these magazines: On page 52, Greg Jennings (5'10" and 195) is described as "lacking bulk," while LSU's Skylar Green, who is shorter and lighter at 5'9" and 193, is described as having "adequate bulk." Another example of ridiculousness is Cutler's scouting report, in which he is described as "lacking elite zip" and having "tools" that aren't "outstanding," whereas I think history has borne out the fact that Cutler's arm and "tools" may in fact be the only "outstanding" thing about him.

5. There's something distinctly Mad-Libby about these scouting reports, especially if you read more than a few in a row. They're all some variety of words, including "upside," "value," "ceiling," "floor," "knee-bender," "waist-bender," "stiff," "fluid," "long speed," and "more quick than fast."

What's even more interesting is thinking about how players from the 2006 class who are still in the league are perceived today. Leinart and Young are, for all intents and purposes, gone (I know, Young just signed with the Browns, but it's more of a "he's basically done, but we need another body for minicamp" kind of a signing at this point). Brodie Croyle, Whitehurst, and Kellen Clemens have all experienced their moment of "maybe he'll be our guy!" but are all also essentially done.

What's odd is how Cutler has survived with his perception of "youngish guy with upside" still intact, even though it's been eight years since 2006 and he really hasn't done much in the postseason or statistically to merit this perception.

Another guy in the same "somehow-clinging-to-young-explosive-upside-guy-perception" category is Reggie Bush. Classmates Laurence Maroney and LenDale White are done. Joseph Addai had moments, even years, of real productivity but is basically done, and Brian Calhoun (second-round grade according to ESPN) never got started. Even role players like Jerious Norwood and Jerome Harrison have long since come and gone. DeAngelo Williams is perceived as getting a little long in the proverbial running back tooth, though he's by far been the best of the class.

So why do we perceive Bush as still young, explosive, and possessing of an upside such that Detroit has pinned its running games hopes (at least in part) on him when we would call Joseph Addai "used up" and DeAngelo Williams "getting old"? Ditto for Cutler, for whom the "upside" beacon still shines bright. Football people, help me understand what I'm missing.

I, of course, have ideas, one being that so much money has been sunk into the contracts of Cutler and Bush that teams are essentially locked into being enthusiastic about them year in and year out because they have no other financial options, even though there's not a whole lot that's quantifiable to get excited about. Another idea is that the Reggie Bush Kool-Aid was so comprehensive in 2006 that it has just sort of carried him this far.

THE NEW ENGLAND APPROACH:
COMPARABLE IN THE AGGREGATE

Perhaps the only way in which *Moneyball* principles truly translate in a football context is the idea of re-creating a particular player's production in the aggregate. Bill Belichick and the New England Patriots have done this at the running back position—a position in which they have traditionally invested very little in terms of money or draft choices. As I'll examine in more detail later in the book, the Patriots, despite being perceived as Tom Brady's pass-first offense, are usually in the top half of the league in carries per game. The Patriots like to run the football and, when they are able to do it well, open up more possibilities for Brady. They have done it without stars at the running back position.

I wrote the following right after New England acquired LeGarrette Blount the first time in a trade with the Tampa Bay Buccaneers:

> I believe that the most significant move made in this year's NFL Draft took place between the New England Patriots and the Tampa Bay Bucs and involved a big back. The Patriots dealt track guy/running back Jeff Demps to the Bucs in exchange for their unhappy running back LeGarrette Blount. Here are the vitals on Blount:
>
> > Height: 6'0" Weight: 247 Career yards: 1,939 Yards per carry: 4.6 Age: 26
>
> Bill Belichick loves a reclamation project and has a deft touch with bad seeds, namely, that he's just not afraid to get rid of them when they've outlived their usefulness (e.g., Randy Moss), and he's not afraid to take them on when they've got something left to give (e.g., Cory Dil-

lon). Blount is in the prime of his career and has a chance to be this offense's iteration of Dillon—a big, physical back that can get the consistent yards that New England has lacked of late. The Patriot offense had become Brady-centric and one-dimensional, and I believe that Blount—a bargain at this price (Demps and a seventh-round pick)—will add this dimension.

Blount has proven to be exactly that, so much so that Belichick acquired him again in 2014 and again for next to nothing—this time after Blount was released by the Pittsburgh Steelers. The Patriots went 12–4 in 2014 and won the Super Bowl. They did it using four ballcarriers—Shane Vereen,[2] Stevan Ridley, Jonas Gray, and Blount. No back on the list had over 500 yards as an individual, but in the aggregate, they had 1,424 yards and as a group averaged 4.2 yards per carry. By comparison, only Dallas's superstar DeMarco Murray had more rushing yards individually than New England's group, and Murray was the focal point of his team's rushing offense. New England's group outrushed stars including LeSean McCoy (1,319), Marshawn Lynch (1,306), Eddie Lacy (1,139), and Arian Foster (1,246).

Of the four backs in New England's rotation, Gray, Blount, and Ridley are all over 220 pounds. By creating a formula that works, Belichick has avoided overpaying for boom-or-bust players like Trent Richardson and even overextending financially to sign a player like Murray. By comparison, when the Saints invested the second-overall pick in the 2006 draft on Reggie Bush, they were getting a player who would never, in a single season, even get close to 1,424 yards rushing. His best was 2011, when he ran for 1,086 yards as a Miami Dolphin. As a Saint, he never rushed for over 600 yards in a single season and didn't average over four yards per carry until his fourth year in the league.

Still, Bush remains in the league while other backs with far better production have come and gone. And there is still the hope that the running back, who is now on his fourth team (San Francisco), can be an "every-down" back in the NFL.

9

THE JOY OF SACKS, PART I

Draft Myths and Projecting Pass Rushers

For what it's worth, the three best single-season sack totals in NFL history were turned in by guys who went to Texas Southern (Michael Strahan), Idaho State (Jared Allen), and East Central Oklahoma (Mark Gastineau). DeMarcus Ware, who appears a little further down the list (twice), went to Troy. Recent Steelers sackmaster James Harrison went to Kent State, and early-2000s sack king Dwight Freeney went to Syracuse. Both Freeney and Harrison fall short of conventional, positional size "requirements," both lacking in what scouts (and television-type scouts) like to call "length." Both went to less-than-powerhouse schools.

The point? All of these stars fell outside a standard industry profile for drafting defensive ends/pass rushers. That profile, simply stated, dictates that for the most part, these players play in the SEC or the Big XII and have certain physical characteristics, including height (6′4″ or above) and long arms.

Given the above, I do find it interesting that there were no non–BCS-conference pass rushers drafted in the top two rounds from 2006 to 2011 (my five-year sample size). I also find it interesting that in the draft season (NFL Combine, all-star games, and Pro Days), scouts continue to be wooed by players who meet a physical profile but fail to translate that profile into college productivity.

Even in my relatively small sample size and relatively quick study, a couple of myths emerged:

Myth #1: Players who fail to record sacks on the college level will somehow, magically, start doing so at the pro level.

The Detroit Lions used their fifth-overall pick in 2013 on a player, Ziggy Ansah, who has length. He's 6'5" with long arms. He ran the right forty-yard-dash time. He also recorded only 4.5 sacks at Brigham Young last season. In this, he reminds me of the following players:

  Quentin Groves, Auburn: Groves, on the strength of some sensational Combine numbers, fit the height/weight/speed profile (mostly speed) and was overdrafted as a result. He had a meager three sacks as a senior at Auburn and has been an NFL bust.
  Robert Ayers, Tennessee: Also overdrafted on the basis of his physical profile, Ayers's best sack output as a college player (four) came in his junior year. He recorded three sacks as a senior. He's been an NFL bust as well.

The Detroit Lions, by nature of their years of futility, are the last team that should be gambling on someone like Ansah, who is drawing comparisons to Jason Pierre-Paul, who has been a difference maker (but, I would argue, not consistently sensational) for the New York Giants. The Lions would have been better served by re-signing Cliff Avril, who at age twenty-seven is in the prime of his career and has already amassed 36.5 NFL sacks. Instead, this is just another example of the Lions being the Lions. Schwartz has a year left to win, and chances are that Ansah won't begin making a significant difference in time to help him save his job.

Myth #2: There's no talent in the Big 10.

While the SEC has produced pass-rush busts like Jarvis Moss, Jamaal Anderson, and Derrick Harvey in the sample period, the Big 10, in the same period, produced the following:

Ryan Kerrigan (Purdue): 16 NFL sacks
Anthony Spencer (Purdue): 32.5 NFL sacks
LaMarr Woodley (Michigan): 52 NFL sacks
Tamba Hali (Penn State): 62.5 NFL sacks

What do all of those players have in common? College productivity. Hali had eleven sacks as a senior at Penn State, Kerrigan had 12.5 as a senior at Purdue (and thirteen the year before). Woodley had twelve in his senior season, and Spencer had 10.5. For what it's worth, Cliff Avril also went to Purdue but fell outside my sample parameters because he was a third-round pick.

The 2013 draft was full of overdrafted/underdrafted players based on what I've written above. Overvalued players include the following:

Barkevious Mingo, LSU: Played a glamour position at a glamour program, fits the physical profile, and was picked high on the basis of a great bowl game and some good workouts. Mingo had 4.5 sacks last season and

disappeared for *long* periods of time (like most of the
regular season) on film. I broke down his Georgia, Auburn, and Mississippi State film, and there's no disputing his explosive first step. Mingo gets out of the blocks
like a sprinter. Interestingly, he spends a lot of time in a
three-point stance, despite his skinny frame, unlike Dion
Jordan (below), who plays almost exclusively from a
two-point. From a production standpoint, Mingo didn't
do a ton, even against Georgia's traditional drop-back
pass offense. He had several one-on-one opportunities
and was generally handled by Georgia's tackles. He did,
however, have a great two-play sequence in which he
had an upfield rush resulting in a sack by a teammate
and then on the following play beat a cut block and then
leapt up and swatted a ball. Mingo and Jordan actually
both remind me a lot of 2015 prospect Randy Gregory.
Dion Jordan, Oregon: Like Mingo, Jordan (6'6") has length
and looks great getting off the bus. Like Mingo, Jordan
wasn't terribly productive in college, collecting five
sacks in 2012. I broke down a few of Jordan's game
tapes from 2012. The first tape I watched was Jordan's
USC game, and, on studying it, I'm not surprised that
scouts loved him. He was a little bulkier than his meas-
urements would indicate, and he showed great length
and burst. Jordan, though his sack production was dubious, had a couple of hurries and some nice plays in
pursuit. His motor looked like it ran a little higher and a
little more often than that of Jadeveon Clowney. Still, it
would be hard to call Jordan "dominant" in any way.
Athletic? Yes. Occasionally a factor? Yes. But certainly
not dominant. More dominant, on the same tape, was

Jordan's Oregon teammate Kiko Alonso, who has been a sleeper hit for the Buffalo Bills.

Undervalued players include the following:

Bjoern Werner, Florida State: Werner was a sack machine in the ACC, collecting thirteen in 2005 and nearly dropping out of the first round because he ran a little slow at the Combine and (let's just say it) is a white guy.

Damontre Moore, Texas A&M: Moore was an absolute steal in the third round, proving that the organizations that consistently play well (like the Giants) also consistently draft well and get value. Moore was a sack machine (8.5 in 2011 and 12.5 in 2012) in two elite conferences (Big 12 and SEC).

As it turns out, I was right on Mingo and Jordan but wrong(ish) on Moore and Werner. Mingo has only seven career sacks in two seasons and has been less impressive than his less talented counterpart at outside linebacker, Paul Kruger, who has collected 15.5 sacks over the same period. Miami's Dion Jordan has been even less impactful, collecting only three sacks in two seasons and starting only one game.

Damontre Moore has been a bit of a disappointment as well, collecting only 5.5 sacks in his first two seasons and not starting a game—though less so because he was just a third-round pick. Werner has collected 6.5 sacks but started every game for Indianapolis in 2014. The Colts are still waiting on him to become a Ryan Kerrigan–like edge player in their 3-4 defense. I evaluated Werner's 2012 North Carolina State tape and saw a player who doesn't do anything particularly freakish from an athletic standpoint but who is extremely sound fundamentally and made some exceptional plays in the run game. Werner showed an ability to stack and shed at the point of attack, and his pursuit down the line was textbook. Despite his lack of freakish Clowneyan athleticism, he was still a hard guy to beat around the corner. He showed good pocket-pushing strength and a nice bull rush, even though opposing tackles routinely outweighed him by fifty pounds or more. Werner will get "hustle" sacks, and some of his sack production may have been a function of playing with a handful of other NFL-quality players on Florida State's front seven. Werner seemed like a little bit of a stretch in the first round, honestly. He seems like a Brooks Reed–type player or, at the low end, a Shea McClellin perhaps.

Ansah, about whom I wrote above, has been an interesting study. He has started twenty-eight games in his first two seasons and has been a difference maker for Detroit. He had eight sacks as a rookie and 7.5 in his sophomore campaign. Still, was he worth a top-five pick in 2013? Maybe, as the rest of that first-round class hasn't really set the world on fire from an impact standpoint. The best players in the 2013 draft came, arguably, out of the second round, including Jonathan Cyprien (166 tackles), D. J. Swearinger, Kiko Alonso, Eddie Lacy, and LeVeon Bell. Both Lacy and Bell have been superstars for their respective clubs.

THE JADEVEON CLOWNEY–ALONZO SPELLMAN DILEMMA: THE ROLE OF THE MEDIA IN CREATING A PROSPECT

South Carolina's Jadeveon Clowney was the most coveted defensive end/pass rusher in the 2014 draft. I wrote the following in the middle of the 2013 college season:

> Houston's J. J. Watt is the reigning king of NFL defensive ends with a rejuvenated Mario Williams, an aging Jared Allen, an on-and-off Julius Peppers, and a cadre of 3-4 outside linebackers who primarily rush the passer also in the discussion.
>
> My first extended 2013 exposure to South Carolina sensation Jadeveon Clowney came this Saturday as South Carolina beat Missouri in an exciting multiple-overtime affair. Clowney, the 6'6", 274-pound, defensive end, is the apple of every television analyst's eye, whether he's making plays or not, as network mandates seem to be, "Talk about Jadeveon Clowney as much as possible." To say that this gets old would be an understatement.
>
> Clowney set South Carolina's sack record last season and was the SEC's defensive player of the year. What's awkward about this season is that though the season is past the halfway point, he only has two sacks. He was shut out against Missouri and in the other Clowney tape I watched versus Tennessee. As I wrote before, when drafting a pass rusher, college sacks usually do portend production at the NFL level. That said, I would be wary to spend a ton of money on a college player without a lot of sack production.
>
> The excuses for Clowney's production run along the lines of "defenses are game-planning for him" and "he's getting chipped and double-teamed." But I would ask, rhetorically, "Do you think defenses didn't chip and double-

team Julius Peppers, J. J. Watt, and other great college pass rushers?"

Simply put, the two game exposures I've had to Clowney this season reveal the same things:

1. There's no disputing his length, first-step quickness, and speed around the edge. These are things that can't necessarily be taught. His size and physical tools put him in "rare physical prodigy" territory also occupied by Peppers, Mario Williams, and very few others. He's also got a sick inside move.

2. Clowney, while very good, has also been the outsized object of media fascination after his helmet-altering hit in last year's Outback Bowl. The hit went viral and made a media legend/superhero out of a guy who is a very good but flawed player.

3. If there had been a way for Clowney to declare for last year's draft, when his stock had been at its highest, that would have been ideal for him. It was almost inevitable that the 2013 season would include a lot of faultfinding.

4. It's hard to run outside to Clowney's side. He gets up-field *real* fast.

5. With his length, Clowney should be a pass-swatting superfreak like Watt. But he isn't. This just seems to be an effort issue, which speaks to the next item.

6. Jadeveon Clowney has a motor problem. He lacks the relentlessness of Watt, Dwight Freeney, and Allen, each of whom collect lots of "effort" sacks and hurries each season. He's not nasty like James Harrison or a physically gifted technician like DeMarcus Ware. He's not overpowering like Reggie White. He plays high. When blocked, Clowney tends to stay blocked. He also appears lackluster in pursuit.

7. I wonder if, with the proliferation of spread schemes and quick-pass offenses, coordinators are rendering players like Clowney semiobsolete? That is, it doesn't

really matter how athletic your defensive end is if I'm lining up in the shotgun and getting the ball out really quickly. Nobody lines up under center in college anymore, and seven-step drops are a relic of the 1980s and 1990s.

Barring a meteoric rise in output, Clowney will turn in a season that is far less productive in terms of numbers than Peppers and Williams had in their final college seasons. It will be decidedly Barkevious Mingo–like, which will create an interesting dilemma for general managers drafting in the top ten. In the 2013 draft, lots of money was spent on relatively unproductive physical freaks like Dion Jordan (third overall), Mingo, and Ziggy Ansah (fifth overall), proving that general managers are still in love with tall, fast defensive ends and will reach for them regardless of production.

Clowney won't be the first-overall pick of the draft and shouldn't be (note: I was wrong—he was). There are too many clubs that need quarterbacks, and there are too many good quarterbacks available. Quantifiably, Marcus Mariota is a better football player than Jadeveon Clowney right now. And he won't dominate and change games at the NFL level as a rookie because he isn't dominating and changing them against Central Florida, North Carolina, and Arkansas this season. That's not to say, "Don't draft Clowney"; it's more to say, "Adjust your expectations." I'd be interested to see Clowney up on his feet as a 3-4 outside linebacker.

So why mention Spellman in the subtitle? Because, like Clowney, he was a physical freak who had a certain man-amongst-boys quality in college. He wasn't an abject bust in the league, but he was never dominant. Chances are that Clowney ends up somewhere in between—a little better than Spellman and, unless he changes his approach, probably never as good as Peppers, Williams, Allen, Freeney, Watt, and others.

As it turned out, Clowney's rookie year was a wash, as he struggled with knee problems and eventually had surgery, causing him to miss most of the season. He ended the 2014 season with seven tackles and no sacks in four games. In December 2014, Clowney had risky microfracture surgery in which tiny fractures are made in the bone underlying cartilage in the knee, which (in theory) causes new cartilage to develop. There is a chance that Clowney will make a full recovery and live up to his potential but probably a better-than-average chance that he will be a very expensive bust.

OVERVALUED IN THE 2015 DRAFT?

Nebraska's Randy Gregory, a defensive end, could be 2015's Barkevious Mingo or Dion Jordan in that he is a player with tantalizing length and speed (at 6'6" and 245) but with dubious sack production as a collegian. Gregory logged only seven sacks in 2014, and 4.5 of them came on back-to-back weeks against a weak Illinois team (2.5) and a mediocre Miami (FL) squad (two). CBS Sports currently has Gregory ranked as their number one defensive end prospect going into the 2015 draft, and he is projected to run in the high 4.4s at the NFL Scouting Combine in February.

I watched Gregory's two-sack performance against Miami and saw a player who does indeed have the speed to be a beast in pursuit but who also didn't seem to be especially violent or creative with his hands. He is a little thin and was frequently redirected by chip blocks. Gregory, like Mingo and Jordan, looks like a small forward on the field and, as such, struggles to "set the edge" on outside runs. However, like Clowney, he shows remarkable strength when he wants to, as some of his most impressive rushes were on "hurries" when he didn't sack the quarterback, the key phrase there being "when he wants to." Like Clowney, he also disappears for stretches at a time despite television's obsession with talking about him. He is handled admirably by Miami's 6′8″ offensive tackle Taylor Gaubois.

That said, one of Gregory's sacks was the kind that makes casual observers drool. In it, he was left unblocked by a confused left tackle, and a very overmatched running back stepped up to try to take him low. Gregory recognized this and hurdled the back on his way to engulfing Kaaya for the sack. It looked great on television but was his first significant play of the game. "You're looking at a first-rounder," said the talking head.

The Miami–Nebraska tape actually revealed a defensive lineman I like better than Gregory: Miami's Anthony Chickillo. While he plays a different position than Gregory, projecting as an interior lineman, Chickillo shows balance at the point of attack and always seems to be around the football, notching a key fumble recovery for the Hurricanes. Chickillo can stack and shed at the point of attack, making him a stout player against the run. He could play immediately as a true 4-3 hand-in-the-dirt defensive end or perhaps even bulk up and bump inside to play defensive tackle.

The truth about Gregory's tape is that it just wasn't all that impressive. The game came and went, and, as it did, there were many other players who "flashed" a lot more often than Gregory—including Chickillo, Miami quarterback Brad

Kaaya, Duke Johnson, and Nebraska running back Ameer Ab-
dullah (as well as his backup Imani Cross, whom I actually
like better). My sense is that a player who will command top-
ten-pick money and attention should be more of a factor in his
college starts because, if what we believe an NFL team is
"buying" is sacks (from a player like Gregory), it may be safer
and cheaper to buy those sacks someplace else (free agency or
a trade) from a player who you know can deliver said sacks. In
this, the pass-rush function is not unlike the quarterback function offensively. Miami, Cleveland, and Houston have gotten
little from their initial investments in Dion Jordan, Barkevious
Mingo, and Jadeveon Clowney, respectively. They were high-
risk propositions.

In this, the pass rusher has almost become the "franchise
quarterback" on the defensive side of the ball. The media will
often create and christen elite pass rushers when one doesn't
actually exist. Gregory may be a beneficiary of this phenomenon.

For the sake of comparison and for fun, I studied one tape
of a long-ago Nebraska defensive end/outside linebacker/edge
rusher prospect named Broderick Thomas, who had his Nebraska heyday in the late 1980s. Thomas, like Gregory, was a
disruptive force on the edge but had to display his disruptive-
ness against a lot of nontraditional, non–pro-style offenses. In
his era's case, it was Oklahoma's wishbone option attack. I
broke down Thomas's "Game of the Century II" tape against
Oklahoma in 1987. Nebraska came into the game number one
in the nation, while Oklahoma, also undefeated, was number
two. Thomas looked a little bit more like a football player than
Gregory, at 6'4" and 254 pounds. By that, I mean that Gregory, at times, looks like a tremendously athletic power forward

in a football uniform, whereas Thomas just looks like a football player. He looked thick. He was a more consistent run-game anchor and was proficient at taking on the kinds of lead blocks that Oklahoma threw at him.

The tape revealed a few other things we've lost in the past twenty-five years. One is nicknames. Thomas christened himself "The Sandman," which is equal parts—the christening and the actual name—ridiculous and awesome. Nebraska I-back Keith Jones referred to himself as Keith "End Zone" Jones.

Thomas was freakish in pursuit and was freakish on a more consistent basis than Gregory. He seemed to play at a more violent pitch and was just, in general, more of a factor on his defense in that it was clear that Oklahoma game-planned away from him at times. When the Sooners ran at him, he anchored and made plays. He didn't have opportunities to make sacks because Oklahoma rarely threw the ball. Just as Gregory will be, Thomas was a high-first-round draft choice, being selected with the sixth pick in the 1987 draft by the moribund Tampa Bay Bucs. According to Armen Keteyian's account in *Big Red Confidential*, "In true Thomas fashion he began wearing an all-leather warmup suit, toting around a cellular phone, cruising the town in his customized Mercedes and Jeep, and signing his name $andman."[1]

Thomas's pro production falls somewhere in between "disappointment" and "star." He collected 47.5 career sacks, which is no small accomplishment, but he wasn't the "next Lawrence Taylor" type–prospect that teams in that era coveted. He played nine total seasons, and had an 11 sack year in 1991 as a Tampa Bay Buc.

Missouri's Shane Ray, who projects (perhaps like Gregory) as a 3-4 outside linebacker at the next level, notched thirteen sacks in 2014, and his production was much more evenly distributed. While Gregory was shut out in six contests (and missed two other games), Ray was much more of a consistent factor, as he played a full season and was shut out only three times and notched multiple-sack games against SEC foes Florida, South Carolina, and Kentucky. Ray also flew a little further under the mainstream media radar, perhaps because his dimensions (6'3" and 245) are a bit less freakish.

Ray's relentlessness is on display early in the Buffalo Wild Wings Bowl, as he gets a piece of a sack in Minnesota's first series. He clearly plays with his motor geared higher than Gregory's and seems more creative in his pass rush. In this (high motor and undersized), he is not unlike a few other recent NFL sack artists who flew under the radar at less-than-marquee programs and lacked size. James Harrison of Kent State was undersized (6'0" and 240 in college) but ultra-productive, leading the Golden Flashes with fifteen sacks in 2001. He went undrafted but currently has 71.5 career NFL sacks and doesn't appear to be slowing down despite his advanced age. Dwight Freeney of Syracuse was 6'1" and 266 coming out of college, where he reportedly was clocked at 4.4 seconds in the forty-yard dash. Another ultra-productive college player, Freeney left Syracuse with thirty-four quarterback sacks and was a unanimous first-team All-American following his senior season. He was drafted with the eleventh selection of the first round of the 2002 NFL Draft and recorded 110 sacks as a professional. He was a seven-time Pro Bowler and a Super Bowl champion.

So how do relatively similar players—both smallish, both ultra-productive—have such disparate 2002 draft experiences? The list of disappointing defensive ends (and, for that matter, outside linebackers) drafted in front of Harrison is extensive and includes names like Kalimba Edwards, Eddie Freeman, Anton Palepoi, Saleem Rasheed (outside linebacker), and Dennis Johnson. All these players were, for whatever reason, less suited to rushing the passer on the pro level than an under-sized and undrafted tweener from the MAC. Kalimba Edwards is a great example of the "power conference/physical attributes" school of scouting. He played at South Carolina and fit the "ideal" NFL size profile at 6'6" and 265 but had only 3.5 sacks as a college senior. He played seven NFL seasons, and his best sack total was 2005, when he recorded seven.

So what are the lessons for 2015? If I'm an NFL club, I'm avoiding what I call the "small forward phenomenon." If a player plays and seems like he's more suited for an NBA uniform than an NFL one, I'm skeptical. These players—like Mingo, Jordan, Clowney, and Gregory—are phenomenal on the stopwatch and look amazing getting off the bus, but their production has been dubious, and that scares me.

10

RETHINKING THE NFL DRAFT

A New Perspective on Player Acquisition

When I was a kid, my parents had a strict "you can only stay home from school if you're puking" rule that they routinely waived one day per year: draft day. In the 1980s, before the draft was the big-business, televised-entertainment juggernaut that it is today, portions of it were conducted on weekdays, and my parents would let me stay home to watch coverage on ESPN. Today, the event not only is covered by ESPN and the NFL Network but has also been moved to prime-time evening slots and spaced over a number of days to accommodate the most viewers. NFL Draft magazines, blogs, and "scouting" services proliferate online as, it seems, everybody wants a piece of the NFL Draft revenue pie. In addition, player scouting has taken on an almost mythic reputation—as anyone who's ever spent more than a few minutes inside an NFL scouting department now has a draft blog or "newsletter" that they're promoting.

Draft entertainment's first megastar was a character named Mel Kiper Jr., who has served as niche NFL Draft analyst for ESPN since 1984. Kiper famously started a draft report service in 1978 and, the first time he offered it to the public in 1981, sold a mere 130 copies. By the mid-1980s, he was a fixture on ESPN's draft telecasts, and his name would appear frequently in predraft media. And, interestingly, as oversaturation is the hallmark of almost every media talking head today—including Kiper heirs apparent Todd McShay (ESPN) and Mike Mayock (NFL Network)—Kiper seems to "save himself" primarily for draft season, and his only real televised "product" is his "Big Board," which ranks only twenty-five players. The fact of the matter is that neither Kiper nor McShay are especially great at getting it right when it comes to predicting NFL success—probably no better or worse than any fan with access to games and information. But that's not why they exist primarily. Both are good entertainment in an entertainment business. To wit, both Kiper and McShay had future megabusts Matt Leinart and Vince Young in their top tens in 2006, but so did a lot of other people, including, apparently, the Cardinals and Titans.

The bigger and more interesting point to the Kiper discussion, however, is the fact that media and fan obsession with the draft may in fact skew our perceptions of how good teams are built. Conventional wisdom since the draft became televised entertainment in the 1980s is that "good teams are built through the draft." It's a bit of football rhetoric that we have a tendency to blindly accept in part because we hear it so often and in part because all football fans love the draft. However, immersion in the world of 1978's NFL is showing me that the draft, while not an afterthought in 1978, seemed to be a far less important ingredient in roster building back then.

We assume that 2014's best teams were built through the draft, but were they? I examined the 2014 rosters of the two best teams (New England Patriots and Seattle Seahawks) and the two worst teams (Tampa Bay Buccaneers and Tennessee Titans) to get a sense for how they were built.

There's no debating the fact that the Patriots have drafted really, really well over the years, and the study bears this out. Franchise cornerstones Tom Brady, Vince Wilfork, Stephen Gostkowski, Rob Gronkowski, Nate Solder, and Chandler Jones were all draft choices. All told, thirty-eight members of the Super Bowl champion Patriots came by way of the NFL Draft or as undrafted college free agents. However, there is another side to this story, particularly for the Patriots. Several key contributors, including Brandon Browner, Brandon La-Fell, LeGarrette Blount, Dan Connolly, Rob Ninkovich, and Darrelle Revis, came from other clubs via free agency. Twenty-six current Patriots came via free agency, trades, or waivers.

Similarly, the Super Bowl runners-up Seahawks acquired thirty players via the NFL draft and ten more as undrafted college free agents—including key wide receivers Doug Baldwin and Jermaine Kearse. However, one could argue that the heart of Seattle's roster came via free agency, where the club added defensive stalwarts Cliff Avril and Michael Bennett to play alongside backfield workhorse Marshawn Lynch, who came via a trade with the Buffalo Bills.

Both teams, without a doubt, have built primarily through the draft, but the Patriots in particular have allowed other NFL teams to "develop" talent that they have then harvested. The worst club in 2014—Tampa Bay—would seem to support the "great teams are built through the draft" conventional wisdom by showing the reverse to be true. The Bucs have drafted very poorly. For one thing, they don't have a player on their roster who was drafted by the team before 2009. And only twenty-four of the the team's current roster players came via the draft or college free agency.

The other bottom dweller of 2014, the Tennessee Titans, are a bit harder to pin down. The Titans brought in a Patriot-like thirty-two players through the draft or college free agency, proving that they may be overcommitted to players in their own program who are underperforming.

For the sake of adding to what might be 2014-related confusion, let's look at the Indianapolis Colts—widely considered to be a team on the rise, building around the arm of franchise quarterback Andrew Luck. The Colts, interestingly, have only nineteen drafted players on their current roster—putting them on par with the putrid Tampa Bay Bucs. They've signed another handful of undrafted free agents, only one of whom (receiver Griff Whalen) is a significant contributor. Interestingly, the Colts have been mega-active in the free agent, trade, and waivers market—adding an astonishing total of forty-one players by those means. The philosophy of the Colts, to some degree, seems to be to let other teams acquire and vet potential players before they are ultimately assimilated in the Colts system. The Colts acquired leading rushers Daniel Herron and Ahmad Bradshaw in free agency from Cincinnati and New York, respectively. Their best cornerback, Vontae Davis, came via a trade with Miami. Contributors Jack Doyle (tight end), A. Q. Shipley (guard), and Shaun Phillips (linebacker) were all waiver-wire pickups.

Culturally, the draft has become something that teams "win or lose" at, and, in fact, a favorite postdraft journalistic exercise is "grading" each team's draft selections. That said, I think we've imbued the draft with more importance than we should given what it actually is: just one of several ways to acquire the kinds of players who can do what your system asks them to do in the best possible way. Models exist of good teams and coaches who have basically eschewed the draft as too risky and who have set about bringing in players by other means.

George Allen's career record as head coach was 116–47 (.712), making him one of the winningest coaches of all time. For the sake of perspective, Bill Walsh's career record was 92–59 (.609), and Bill Belichick's is 211–109 (.659). Both led dynasties, and both are deserving of the "legendary" tag. Neither won quite as often as Allen.

What's interesting about Allen is that he disdained the NFL Draft and chose instead to build his winning rosters with players who were usually older and almost always came from somewhere else. To wit, on his 1972 squad, which represented the NFC in the Super Bowl, Allen had only eight starters (out of twenty-two) who were drafted by the Redskins, and none of those eight were selected by Allen and his regime. The other fourteen players were acquired either via waivers or in trades with other squads. Allen was especially fond of trading draft choices for established players. He brought in players like Pat Fischer, Jack Pardee, and Verlon Biggs this way, leaving him with drafts like the 1972, draft in which his club didn't pick until the eighth round and had only two players from said draft who ever suited up for the club. Truth be told, most of Allen's drafts were like this. In his 1977 draft, two players made the squad, and he didn't have a pick until the fourth round.

In a unique way, Allen saw the entire league as his draft pool, and he saw the "draft" as an ongoing experiment in which players who fit his system could always be purchased in exchange for picks. In this way, he was making investments in players who had already been vetted by the league and found acceptable. There's an interesting logic in this approach, and I wonder why more teams don't do it. Perhaps it's because we've fallen in love with the idea of "winning" at the draft to such a degree that we've forgotten that everyone is for sale all the time for the right price. It makes me wonder how many teams passed on trading for current Seahawk superstar Marshawn Lynch in favor of finding a running back in the draft.

Jon Gruden's draft record in Oakland and Tampa Bay is similar in some interesting ways. Although he is considered an offensive guru and is a practitioner of the West Coast offense made famous by the king of quarterbacks, Joe Montana, Gruden never drafted a franchise quarterback in his eleven years as an NFL head coach. And, interestingly, the Super Bowl–winning 2002 Bucs roster that he inherited from Tony Dungy was itself a study in Dungy's draft philosophy. The offense, with the exception of guard Cosey Coleman, fullback Mike Alstott, and tackle Kenyatta Walker, was made up entirely of castoffs from other teams. Brad Johnson was drafted by the Vikings, Michael Pittman was a former Arizona Cardinal, and leading receivers Keyshawn Johnson and Keenan McCardell were Jets and Redskins, respectively.

The defense, however, was an entirely different story, as it was populated by stars and future Hall of Famers (Derrick Brooks and Warren Sapp) drafted before or during the Dungy regime. In his tenure as the head coach of the Indianapolis Colts, Dungy made a dozen first- and second-round selections between 2002 and 2008, and only two of the first-round picks were used on offensive players (wide receiver Anthony Gonzales and running back Joseph Addai). Dungy, generally, drafted the positions that tended to be "safest," using high picks on defensive players like Dwight Freeney, Larry Tripplett, Tim Jennings, and Bob Sanders.

GAMING THE NFL DRAFT?

Gaming the NFL Draft has become a cottage industry, and, as I mentioned before, swing a cat in any direction, and you'll hit a scout or former scout or wannabe scout touting a system or new metric that will "revolutionize" the draft process. Since *Moneyball*, guys like me have spent way too much time trying to figure out how to reduce the riskiness of the draft when, in fact, deemphasizing the draft may be the only way to really do so. The draft—especially the early rounds of the draft—is far and away the riskiest way to acquire an NFL player.

Undrafted free agency is less risky because it's cheap. There's little to no guaranteed money involved in bringing in a Kurt Warner, Wes Welker, James Harrison, or Jeff Saturday for a workout. I was a high school kid working as a ball boy in Indianapolis when an unknown basketball player from Bradley University named Marcus Pollard showed up at training camp wearing a tank top, accompanied by his agent at the time, who looked to be only a year or two older. Pollard asked for a workout and got one. The team told him to come back in a year when he had added football bulk. It was 1994. He did, and he ended up playing until 2008, catching 349 NFL passes in the process. Of course, for every Pollard, there are countless others who don't make it.

Free agency and trades are less risky because, at some level, everyone involved is a proven commodity. Trading a pick for a proven player is, on paper (injuries and so on excluded), just another way of "spending" that pick. Now, as in the case of Trent Richardson to the Colts, that can still go wrong. But it went wrong primarily because Richardson hadn't really even proved himself in Cleveland. Acquiring him was still a speculative endeavor.

A modern example of the perfect trade scenario was St. Louis acquiring Marshall Faulk in 1999. The Rams knew that Faulk would play a key role in their wide-open offense and brought him in for the relatively cheap price of second- and fifth-round draft choices. Instead of languishing in a Colts offense that wasn't quite right for him, Faulk flourished in St. Louis, posting the best statistical seasons of his career, going to four Pro Bowls (as a Ram), and playing a key role as a ballcarrier and receiver on a Super Bowl champion in his first season as a Ram (1999).

And how did the Colts spend those picks? On a middling starting linebacker in Mike Peterson, who had a good but not great career, and a rotation defensive lineman in Brad Scioli. I'm sure if they could do this one over again, they would do things differently.

A closer look at that 1999 Rams roster reveals a team whose key parts came via means other than the NFL Draft. Warner was, of course, the league's most famous undrafted free agent and is now in the Hall of Fame. Faulk came via trade. Starting center Mike Gruttadauria was an undrafted free agent, and the two guards beside him, Adam Timmerman and Tom Nutten, came via Green Bay and Buffalo, respectively. The heart and soul of the defense, London Fletcher, was another undrafted free agent, and the last-play hero of the Super Bowl, Mike Jones, was first an Oakland Raider.

So does this mean that the draft is unimportant? Of course not. It simply means that there is more than one way to build an NFL team and that often, in today's "win now" NFL, coaches and general managers end up drafting players for the coaches and general managers who will follow them. The draft is great televised entertainment and is now a huge part of the NFL's yearlong ratings-generating calendar. And it's arguably the most fun. But we need to be careful lest we inflate its importance.

WEEK FIVE: DETROIT AT EDMONTON: THE SIGNATURE WIN (AND AN INTERVIEW WITH COMMISSIONER BRANDON ROSE)

Every football program needs a signature win, and Detroit got theirs on the road against a superior Edmonton Eskimos team in Week Five. Edmonton rolled into the game undefeated, riding a Mark Van Eeghen–led run game and a very balanced passing attack involving all three wideouts and tight end Bob Tucker. Detroit came in determined to run the ball and got workman-like efforts from Dexter Bussey and backup Kevin Long, who was close to a hundred yards with a score. The Lions also made a renewed commitment to involving tight ends David Hill and Andre Tillman.

"Tillman and Hill both asked for the football this week in practice, and I wanted to reward them," said Kluck after the game. "They responded with a great outing." Hill picked up several key first downs, and Tillman made a seven-yard touchdown grab in the second quarter. "They are both dynamic receivers, and we need to find ways to get them involved."

Lions quarterback Brian Sipe was also coolly efficient, throwing short to Hill, Tillman, and Wes Chandler, who continued his dazzling rookie year with six catches for ninety yards.

Defensively, the Lions harassed Edmonton quarterback Joe Theismann all afternoon, sacking and hurrying the former Notre Dame star and forcing repeated bad throws. Detroit got two interceptions from Willie Alexander and another from veteran trade acquisition (and former Edmonton Eskimo) Roger Wehrli. Another trade pickup, defensive end Cedric Hardman, collected three tackles and two sacks. "We switched Cedric from right side to the left side of the formation this week," Kluck explained. "He looked much more comfortable." Linebacker Jim Merlo had a pair of sacks in the victory as well.

The Lions, at times, played like a team with nothing to lose, going for it three times on fourth down and converting twice. Kluck has been called a "riverboat gambler" by his peers.

"It was a total team victory," said Kluck of the 26–10 win. "We're going to enjoy it tonight and then start preparing for Philadelphia."

Brandon, Edmonton's coach, grew increasingly frustrated during the game, as things continued to go my way. "All of the crap that usually happens to me is happening to you," I messaged him during the game. It was true in that many of the fumbles and interceptions and random, negative acts of chance that typically mark my games went against him this time. Still, we coached a pretty rock-solid game—we including my son,

Tristan, who has taken up permanent residence at my left elbow during these games and whose football acumen and eyeballs have proven invaluable.

"You should blitz Peters," he reminded me in the third quarter of my run-stopping stud safety, who is a liability in pass coverage. He was right. We reaped the benefit. "Try a medium fade to Chandler," he said when he noticed that Edmonton was crowding the line of scrimmage and showing blitz. Chandler was single-covered. My son has a mind for football and the mental quickness to make these decisions in thirty-second windows.

Despite Brandon's frustration at losing, he was gracious enough to talk about his draw to retro sim leagues:

> I believe the simple answer to what interested me in a retro football sim league is the opportunity to coach and game-plan against my childhood heroes. Action! PC Football allows you to do this. The idea behind me starting the Odyssey Football League and making the inaugural season 1960 was just that. My earliest memories of football [he was born in 1953] are around 1960. I can still remember those Sundays when the Packers [growing up in Milwaukee] game was our NFL game, and later Sunday afternoon, my brother and I would watch the AFL [American Football League] game. My Dad would laugh at the AFL games. He'd tell us it was a second-rate league with second-rate players. He laughed and laughed when the Denver Broncos played a season with vertical striped socks. I can still hear him saying, "They look like a bunch of girls!"

I ask Brandon how his involvement in historical sim leagues has informed his viewing and enjoyment of present games. Specifically, I wonder if there is something the modern

NFL is missing based on his involvement in its past (either cultural or strategic):

> Being a football fan from the 1960s to today, it is so apparent how the game has gravitated towards the passing game, which makes football a more wide-open game than the one I grew up with. It has devalued running. As a kid I loved the AFL because of all of the passing and how wide open their games were, especially the Houston Oilers [George Blanda and company] and San Diego Chargers [Sid Gillman] games. Being older, I wish the game would revert back to its roots and be more balanced. Let the defenses play defense. Make running the ball important again.

I think the NFL pendulum will eventually swing back to a more balanced if not run-oriented style of play if only because colleges are no longer producing NFL-ready quarterbacks and there is less risk involved in a run-oriented system. It's one of the theories I'm trying to prove via my involvement in Brandon's league:

> As far as the actual stadium experience goes, in the old days we went to a football game for the game. Today [being a Dolphins season ticket holder], it seems there are more and more people at the games for the social side [tailgating, drinking, and acting stupid] instead of cheering on the home team.

I'm reminded that, in the end, much of what is good about football is what takes place between fathers and sons. Many of my memories of the game, as a player and a fan, revolve around my father and his opinions on teams, players, and schemes. Hours are spent discussing these things because they are, at some level, safe:

We know how the AFL story ended. My dad died [leukemia] in 1965, so he never got to see how it all played out. I have a feeling he would have been surprised. Weren't most of the NFL establishment fans? Our generation embraced the AFL and the differences to a great game that it offered. Like more passing, African Americans dominating rosters, players' names on the backs of the jersey, the Chiefs huddle, the first soccer-style kicker, different cities/nicknames, etcetera.

The AFL pulled off what no rival league has been able to since—which is make enough of a run at enough good players that the NFL could not merely crush it (e.g., USFL and XFL) but had to assimilate it. Perhaps the ultimate AFL moment was Joe Namath calling his shot and guaranteeing Super Bowl III before going out and making good on that guarantee. His signature trot off the field, waving his index finger in the air, has become a part of professional football lore in part because of how it was captured on film. Like many of us in the league, Brandon has an extensive collection of past-oriented NFL ephemera and finds himself increasingly drawn to the retro stuff over current league coverage:

I have a decent DVD library of NFL and AFL stuff from the past, mostly team season highlights and championship games. I also have an extensive book and periodical library of all kinds of NFL and AFL stuff. That includes the entire collection of *Street & Smith's College and Pro Football Yearbooks* from 1940 to 2007, when they ceased operation. As we meander through the past, I pull out those books or periodicals to read what was being written about the teams and players. We know how all of their careers played out, so I find what the experts wrote while they were playing to be awfully fascinating.

Fascinating indeed. I bought an old copy of *Petersen's Pro Football 1978 Annual*. In it, then–Colts coach Ted Marchibroda says of my quarterback, Bert Jones, "I'm not too sure Bert didn't accomplish more with less to work with than he had in '76. Because of injuries, more responsibility was put on his shoulders and I thought he came through for us."

I can hear Marchibroda's unique, grandfatherly delivery and measured words as I read the quote. He was one of my first "real" bosses, as I worked one summer as a Colts ball boy when Marchibroda was nearing the end of his coaching career in 1994. It was a strange confluence of eras given that Marchibroda's résumé includes players like Jones, but in 1994, it would also include a rookie running back and future Hall of Famer named Marshall Faulk. Marchibroda was the first football coach to whom I was exposed in my brief eighteen years who treated football players like men. It's become cliché to call coaches "professorial," and he wasn't exactly that either; rather, he just created an environment that seemed exceedingly *professional*, and his players (which included future coaching sensation Jim Harbaugh) seemed to respond. But really what remembering Marchibroda reminds me is that I am now old enough to have significant memories, to spin yarns. I am turning into my own father.

11

SCOUTING PARADIGMS

From 1978 to Today

As I type this, I'm watching a live video feed of the Clemson University Pro Day, as Pro Days have become must-see pre-draft television for football nerds such as myself. For the uninitiated, the Pro Day involves colleges hosting all of the NFL scouts, who just a few weeks previous were in Indianapolis for the NFL Scouting Combine. The scouts traverse the nation to see prospects doing the exact same drills they were doing a few weeks ago in Indianapolis, except that they are doing the drills on their own indoor-facility FieldTurf as opposed to the FieldTurf at Lucas Oil Stadium in Indianapolis. I am watching gigantic black men in tight purple spandex "onesies" doing events like the broad jump and the vertical jump and being weighed and measured under the watchful eye of largely white, largely doughy NFL scouts. The collection of both muscle tone and tattoos is astonishing.

The slave-trade parallels are so obvious as to not even really bear mentioning. To say that it's weird would also be a massive understatement. This is the present and the future of NFL scouting.

A newly thin and newly minted Buffalo Bills head coach Rex Ryan is on camera in a Bills windbreaker, doing what Rex Ryan does best—telling a story about unearthing Jets star line-backer Bart Scott at Southern Illinois and then guffawing with the ESPN3 talking heads. They love him. He recently traded star linebacker Kiko Alonso to Philadelphia for star running back LeSean McCoy and is basking in the glow of said trade. One of the talking heads says "Jagwires" when trying to say "Jacksonville Jaguars." He then says, "As fans, we think this is a game. This is a business."

The camera pans to three clinically obese scouts huddled near each other, all wearing officially licensed team gear and all furiously scribbling in loose-leaf notebooks. There is something distressingly genital-centric about the purple Clemson onesies.

An offensive guard named David Beasley bench presses 225 pounds twenty-five times. A defensive end pumps out seventeen reps, and the on-screen graphic indicates that his major is "Community Recreation." Most NFL talent evaluators, if pressed, would admit that this particular metric is completely meaningless, as is, probably, much of what happens at these Pro Days. The camera zooms in close to record each player's pained grimace as they strain under the weight of the bar.

In 1978, two of the NFL's most statistically dominant quarter-backs were Seattle's Jim Zorn, who compiled 3,283 passing yards, and Pittsburgh's Terry Bradshaw, who led the league with twenty-eight touchdown passes. Their two paths to stardom were in some ways similar, as both came from smaller, under-the-radar colleges—Zorn from Cal Poly–Pomona and Bradshaw from Louisiana Tech. Zorn was an undrafted free agent, and Bradshaw was the "franchise" on whom the Steelers pinned their hopes when they made him the first-overall pick in the 1970 NFL Draft.

Bradshaw's first five seasons were up and down to say the least. He held a tenuous grasp on the starting job, and completed over 50 percent of his passes only once (1971) between 1970 and 1974. He was booed mercilessly and reviled by the media in his own city. Bradshaw was called "stupid" and "a country bumpkin," and there were doubts as to whether he could lead an NFL offense. Of course, four Super Bowls, three Pro Bowls, and one Hall of Fame induction later, those doubts have been dispelled. Bradshaw, in part by the nature of his playing résumé as well as his long and successful television career, is a household name.

Zorn came to Seattle in 1976 and started immediately. In some ways, his early struggles paralleled those of Bradshaw. He struggled mightily to complete passes (47 and 41 percent in his first two seasons) and threw more interceptions than touchdowns in both years. Then, in 1978, the tide turned. His team had the first winning season in the history of the franchise, and Zorn, in the ensuing years, would become the "face" of that franchise, along with Steve Largent.

In 1978, Chicago's Walter Payton rushed for 1,395 yards and eleven touchdowns—this following a 1977 season in which he set a league record for rushing yards in a single game (275 vs. Minnesota) and rushed for a whopping 1,852 yards and fourteen touchdowns. Payton was drafted fourth overall in 1975 out of tiny Jackson State University.

Another Jackson State alum, Houston linebacker Robert Brazile, was perhaps the league's best linebacker. Brazile was selected two picks after Payton, sixth overall, in the 1975 draft. At 6'4" and 241 pounds, the athletic and versatile Brazile would be considered "prototype" today. He played ten seasons, went to seven Pro Bowls, and started every NFL game he was a part of.

Oakland's Ted Hendricks, "The Mad Stork," was one of the league's preeminent outside linebackers despite an odd set of physical dimensions. Hendricks was white, too tall at 6'7", and way too skinny at 220 pounds, yet he started 192 career games and made eight Pro Bowls, including his final season at age thirty-six. How many thirty-six-year-old starting outside linebackers are there in the game today? And how many of the league's starters deviate from a de facto "standard" set of physical dimensions?

Hendricks's contemporary on Oakland's defensive line, Otis Sistrunk, didn't even play college football and didn't begin playing professionally until age twenty-six. Hall of Fame Raider corner Willie Brown played at Grambling.

The 1978 AFC Pro Bowl representative at defensive end was Denver's Lyle Alzado. Alzado was a fourth-round pick out of tiny Yankton College in South Dakota—a school that shortly thereafter eliminated its football program entirely. His Pro Bowl counterpart at defensive end? Houston's Elvin Bethea, who was an eight-time Pro Bowler and Hall of Famer from North Carolina A&T.

My own tight end, David Hill, a Pro Bowler in 1978, played collegiately at Texas A&M–Kingsville—not exactly a pipeline to pro football stardom. Two of the league's best cornerbacks in the mid- to late 1970s were both old (over thirty) and white—Pat Fischer and Roger Wehrli.

Why do I share these anecdotes? To illustrate the fact that in today's scouting and media environment, many of those fantastic players either wouldn't have received an opportunity at all or certainly wouldn't have been drafted as high as they were, which is ironic given the massiveness of the time and budgets that are thrown at scouting today. Bradshaw would have been dinged for "inferior" college competition. Ditto for Payton, Brazile, Hill, Bethea, Brown, and Alzado. Sistrunk, most likely, wouldn't have been discovered at all.

And if Bradshaw had somehow made it out of Louisiana Tech and into the first round in today's environment, his franchise certainly wouldn't allow him five years to develop. Quarterbacks like Christian Ponder and Blaine Gabbert were barely given a full sixteen games before their teams bailed on them.

Ted Hendricks, to the naked eye, looks too skinny and oddly shaped to play professional football. He would have probably failed to bench 225 for reps at the Scouting Combine and would have plummeted accordingly in the draft. And the likelihood of a Jim Zorn—an undrafted free agent from a small school being tabbed to start from day one—is slim to none. More likely, he would have, if anything, been mired on a practice squad and then released with barely a mention on the fine print of a local sports page.

The NFL Scouting Combine as we know it today began in 1982 as the brainchild of Tex Schramm, the president and general manager of the Dallas Cowboys, as a way to centralize information for NFL clubs. Prior to 1982, teams scheduled individual visits with players to run them through drills (these things still happen, a bit of overkill?). Officially called the National Invitation Camp, the Combine was organized by a scouting collective called National Football Scouting, Inc., which served as an informational clearinghouse for member teams who subscribed to their service. At the time, there were a couple of other rival camps that were soon assimilated, resulting in what we now call the Combine. Players attend and participate by invitation only.

The Combine was first aired on television in 2004—not surprisingly, a year after the launch of the NFL Network, which has exclusive non-ESPN access to the event. Prior to 2004, the Combine was conducted under a semi-amusing cloak of secrecy in which media and cameras were historically barred. In 2010, the network aired over thirty hours of Combine footage and drew 5.24 million viewers.

Like all things overexposed, the Combine has become a bit of a self-parody in recent years and is as much a fashion show (a showcase for men's spandex provider Under Armour) and media circus as an actual football event. Critics rightly point out that players will rarely, if ever, be asked to run forty yards in a straight line in their careers, and if they can play football, who cares? Terrell Suggs, a star outside linebacker from Arizona State, ran a very pedestrian 4.83 and was summarily downgraded as a result, sliding to the tenth-overall pick in the 2003 draft. He is now Baltimore's all-time sack leader with 106.5 and counting.

At the Combine, players are tested in the bench press (225 for reps), the forty-yard dash (which has become must-see television), the broad jump, the vertical jump, the three-cone agility drill, the twenty- and sixty-yard shuttles, and positional drills. In addition, and perhaps more important, players are given a battery of injury evaluations and medical screenings on the logic that if teams are purchasing them for the next several years in order to play a violent game, they had better not arrive with a previously hidden injury.

Needless to say, in 1978, scouts operated without such luxuries and did so on a much smaller budget. So one would assume that their results would be shakier—more busts, fewer successful drafts—than today. Not necessarily.

The first round of the 1978 NFL Draft saw twenty-eight players selected, and, for it being the supposed scouting "dark ages," teams did remarkably well in making their selections. The first round of the 1978 draft was relatively loaded with stars, like Earl Campbell, Mike Kenn, Clay Matthews, James Lofton, Wes Chandler, John Jefferson, and Ozzie Newsome. Newsome, Lofton, and Campbell are all in the Hall of Fame. It also had its share of solid starters, like Doug Williams, who was the first African American quarterback to win a Super Bowl, and solid (if unspectacular) players, like Chris Ward, Ross Browner, Luther Bradley, Reese McCall, Blair Bush, John Anderson, Keith Simpson, Gordon King, and Dan Bunz. The other eleven players—long-forgotten names, like Elvis Peacock, Larry Bethea, and Ken McAfee—can probably safely be called busts. Here are the stats for the 1978 draft:

Stars: seven
Solid starters: ten
Busts: eleven

Let's fast-forward thirty years to the 2008 draft, in an era when the NFL Scouting Combine had become must-see television and NFL teams sent scouts crisscrossing the nation to

Pro Days at every significant college program in the country. By 2008, once-small NFL scouting departments had ballooned to, on average, thirteen scouts and support staff, spending between $2 million and $3 million per year[1] on college and pro scouting.

The 2008 NFL Draft was held in New York's Radio City Music Hall and was broadcast by ESPN and the NFL Network. On ESPN alone, over 34.8 million[2] viewers tuned into draft coverage. A year later, the draft would shift to a prime-time evening format and pull even higher ratings. By 2008, every major sports media outlet had a draft magazine or at least a special issue devoted to the draft and its prospects.

The 2008 draft saw thirty-one players selected in the first round, and, all things considered, it was an up-and-down group, including Pro Bowlers like Jake Long, Ryan Clady, Jerod Mayo, Matt Ryan, Dominique Rodgers-Cromartie, Aquib Talib, Chris Johnson, Mike Jenkins, and Duane Brown. Add to that list a group of solid starters, like Chris Long, Keith Rivers, Jonathan Stewart, Branden Albert, Darren McFadden (who could arguably be on the bust list), Rashard Mendenhall, and the underappreciated Joe Flacco.

The list of 2008 busts, however, is a bit longer. It would include high-pick disappointments, like Glenn Dorsey, Vernon Gholston, Sedrick Ellis, and Derrick Harvey, as well as names like Chris Williams, Jeff Otah, Sam Baker, Felix Jones, Lawrence Jackson, Kentwan Balmer, Antoine Cason, and Dustin Keller, the last of whom played well but saw his career derailed by injuries. All told, the final tally looks something like this:

Stars: Zero? I'm not sure I'd go so far as to say that any of these players are stars. It looked like Matt Ryan might be headed that way before his team took a nosedive in 2013 and 2014. Jake Long is probably the closest thing this group has to a bona fide star, as he made four Pro Bowls to start his career but has tailed since. One thing is for certain: there will be no Hall of Famers in this group.

Solid: Eighteen. This class was marked by a number of players who had freakishly good seasons and then came back down to earth—the most noteworthy of whom is Chris Johnson, who seems like he's been around much longer than he actually has been. By contrast, quarterback Matt Ryan seems "newer" than he actually is. We still perceive him, interestingly, as a young guy with upside, though he is nearing thirty years of age. Still, he has been very good. Ryan has completed 64 percent of his passes and has 181 touchdowns to only ninety-one picks. He is a quarterback whom nearly any franchise would like to have. Other names here include solid New England linebacker Jerod Mayo and solid cornerbacks Aquib Talib and Dominique Rodgers-Cromartie.

Busts: Fourteen. This is a bust-heavy draft class filled with the usual assortment of failed pass rushers, like Vernon Gholston and Derrick Harvey, as well as washout left tackles Chris Williams, Jeff Otah, and Sam Baker. Defensive tackles Kentwan Balmer and Sedrick Ellis were massive disappointments as well.

It would be silly to suggest that one comparison of two drafts is enough data on which to base a statement like the following: the bloated scouting departments and budgets aren't working. But there's probably some truth to it. There were more busts and fewer stars per capita in the 2008 class than the 1978 class in spite of the fact that we have more video, more money, more resources, and more scouting opportunities than ever before. That could speak to the fact that the 2008 crop of players just wasn't as good. But 1978 isn't considered a stellar draft either.

What's telling about 2008 is the number of good players who came out of the second round. The draft's best running back, Matt Forte, was selected with the forty-fourth pick. Its best pass rusher, Arizona Cardinal Calais Campbell, was picked fiftieth. Its best wide receiver, Jordy Nelson, was taken with the thirty-sixth pick. But why so many whiffs in the first round? We may never know. Still, the Combine/Pro Day/draft grind wears on, and scouts continue to congregate, mysteriously, in the middle of the field to "compare" forty-yard dash times, which itself proves that getting an accurate time is probably a pipe dream.

"I'm looking to see how guys compete in the drills," explains former Clemson Tiger and current Arizona Cardinals assistant coach Brentston Buckner on the Pro Day broadcast. "I just want to see how they move. Have they been working? I want to see if they respect the grind. The NFL is a grind." The words "respect the grind" will undoubtedly be on a T-shirt before the day is over.

There is Rob Ryan and his magnificent gray mane of long hair saying, "I'm really excited about these guys."

There is Clemson punter Bradley Pinion explaining, "I do a lot of hot yoga." Talking-head guffawing ensues. He is, like nearly all punters, white and patently uncool.

Legendary Patriots head coach Bill Belichick is on the sidelines in jeans and a button-down shirt, making him better dressed for this event than at any moment during the actual football season. He looks the part of the reigning Super Bowl champion—relaxed and a little bit "above" the actual clipboard-carrying, note-making, time-comparing mass of scout humanity.

The wife of Clemson's head coach, Kathleen Swinney, is beckoned onto camera by the television brass. "He looks so handsome in his suit, doesn't he!" she gushes to the talking head about the other talking head. She speaks with a thick southern accent and is so conventionally pretty that it hurts. She looks the part of the high-profile coach's wife, which is not unlike being the wife of a high-profile politician. "All of our wives love the players," she explains. The talking head explains that Swinney was recently voted the "second hottest wife" in all of college football. She feigns embarrassment and offense but clearly loves this.

Her husband, Dabo Swinney, has built a marquee program at Clemson and has graduated many of his players (over 91 percent). He says of star defensive end Vic Beasley, "He bought in." This is coach-speak for "he did everything we told him to." He says, later, "He's just a football player." He mentions the fact that 81 percent of Clemson alums who have been drafted or invited to NFL camps as free agents have made a roster. This is impressive.

Tomorrow, the same diaspora of scouts will migrate to Arizona State and Northern Illinois.

WEEK SIX: WASTELAND—PHILADELPHIA 19, DETROIT 7

I am amazed at how, when I tell people about this project, they freely volunteer their own memories. An academic colleague and lifelong Bills fan e-mailed, "Use your shadowy Internet source to find me the Roland Hooks game where he made contact with every member of the defense on his way to the end zone. He was the original Beast Mode!" To this, I replied, "I just signed Roland Hooks!" The real Roland Hooks is now sixty-two years old. He is among the players who did nothing for me in Week Six.

Detroit's Week Six loss to Philadelphia was one of those frustrating games in which nobody on either side plays particularly well and nothing is learned. I always hated those games as a real player and a coach—games that seem to come and go with no new insight and seem instead to hinge on randomness and chance. To wit, my defensive game plan included keying on Philly running back Franco Harris, who was arguably Philly's only good offensive skill player. Harris still ran for nearly 100 yards and had several key catches.

Brian Sipe reverted back to his 1977 self, throwing for only 109 yards and an interception. David Hill had one catch for minus one yard. My enigmatic pass rusher Cedric Hardman had no tackles and no sacks this week after a dominant performance last week. All of the things we did offensively against a superior team last week didn't work this week against an inferior team. It was maddening. We felt the loss of left tackle Mike Wilson, who was injured last week, and fullback Don Hardeman, who went down this week. The story of the game?

I turned the ball over twice, and he didn't. He was less bad than I was. He wins 16–7.

I let my son coach most of the second half, as I was entertaining a friend who was in from Boston and wanted to stick around and see us coach the game. He's a PhD in theoretical mathematics and wanted to know how the game's algorithms worked. His wife is pregnant with their first child, and he wanted to talk about parenting. Real life was encroaching on sim life.

The loss bothers me more than most, as my opponent didn't seem especially gracious. There was none of the usual congenial chat during the game. He simply said, "I need to be done by 6:20." Okay. This bothered me more than it should have. In my strange emotional economy, I'd rather lose to someone nice. There's no explaining the male ego.

12

THE JOY OF SACKS, PART II

Trades and Free Agency

The NFL is brilliant at keeping its product in front of fans throughout the calendar year. Once the Super Bowl wraps up in early February, there is a steady drip of Combine prep, the actual Combine, Pro Days, free agency, and then the NFL Draft in the spring. This season, a few teams seem to be implementing the "draft picks as currency" model.

The struggling Chicago Bears traded enigmatic (difficult, at times crazy) wide receiver Brandon Marshall to the Jets in exchange for a paltry fifth-round draft choice. Marshall's physical skills are breathtakingly unique. He stands 6′4″ and 229 pounds yet had/has legitimate wide receiver speed, making him a matchup nightmare. Marshall had an "off" year in 2014, catching only sixty-one balls in a season that saw much of the Chicago roster visibly give up in several games. It was a season that also saw him at odds with his head coach (the now-fired Marc Trestman) and other teammates. Marshall, from a football standpoint, is your classic mixed bag. The Jets have chosen to risk the "crazy" in hopes of rekindling the career of a player who has caught over 100 balls five out of his nine years in the league. Marshall is legit—especially when he's happy and has bought in to the system. The reality of this trade is that the Jets risked *very* little in exchange for a very good player. Following are players the Jets have acquired with their fifth-round pick in the past five drafts.

Linebacker Jeremiah George has zero NFL starts, and offensive lineman Oday Aboushi has only ten. Fullback John Conner distinguished himself as the star of the Jets' HBO *Hard Knocks* appearance a few years ago and was a favorite of then head coach Rex Ryan but has done little to distinguish himself since. Slot receiver Jeremy Kerley has been a pleasant surprise and solid starter but far from a star. So it makes sense to use a fifth-round choice to purchase a receiver with Marshall's significant pedigree despite his significant baggage. The fifth-round pick has been worth very little.

The Detroit Lions made a similar move in an attempt to replace departed defensive tackle Ndamukong Suh, who left in free agency for a huge payday with the Miami Dolphins. Suh is a rare talent as well—a four-time Pro Bowler and three-time All-Pro who is both uniquely able to anchor in the run game and athletic enough to provide a significant pass rush from the defensive tackle position. He has accrued 181 tackles and thirty-six sacks over a five-year career—astonishing numbers for a defensive tackle. Suh, like Marshall, also came with his fair share of baggage, as he had trouble staying out of the way of officials and has been penalized thirty-five times for a total of 262 yards in his five-year career. I have to think that those 262 penalty yards (not to mention the negative public relations that has come with many of them) have canceled out many of the positive sack yards that Suh has been responsible for in his Detroit tenure. Not that this—by a long shot—is the only metric by which we measure the effectiveness of a defensive tackle, but I'm sure it factored into Detroit's decision to not tie up future money in the enigma that is Suh.

Enter Haloti Ngata. Similar to the Jets deal, the Lions dealt a fourth- and fifth-round pick to Baltimore in exchange for the aging but still very effective Ngata. They get a player who is a machine against the run and who has been to the Pro Bowl four out of the past five seasons. At 6′4″ and 335, Ngata is a different player than Suh and lacks the latter's pass-rush explosiveness but is still an elite defensive tackle who comes at a very low (pickwise) price. Detroit has been even more ho-hum than the Jets with their fifth-round selections over the past several years. Of the five players they've drafted, one (Doug Hogue) is out of the league, and the remaining four have only fifteen starts among them. Of their six fourth-round selections over the same time period, only Sammie Lee Hill has made significant starts, and he is now a Tennessee Titan.

The question is, why aren't more teams making similar deals, and why aren't the price tags higher for established, quality players like Ngata and Marshall? I think it's because we still tend to overvalue the college draft.

LICENSE TO DRIVE

Earlier, we looked at where sacks come from and the trickiness of acquiring pass rushers. Now I want to examine how much they're actually worth on the field.

I took a look at the team sack numbers for 2014, expecting to find elite teams like New England and Seattle near the top. What I found instead is a much-improved albeit still not playoff-worthy Buffalo Bills squad leading the league in sacks with fifty-four. Also in the top ten were the disappointing Giants (forty-seven), Chiefs (forty-six), Jets (forty-five), and the moribund Jacksonville Jaguars (forty-five). The Patriots were all the way down the list at number thirteen with forty sacks, and the supposedly vicious Seattle pass rush collected only thirty-seven sacks in 2014—good for twentieth in the league.

The same study for 2013 yielded similar results. Topping the list were Carolina with sixty sacks, the Bills with fifty-seven, and the Rams with fifty-three. None of those teams made the playoffs. The Rams led the league in sacks (fifty-two) in 2012 as well, but for all their collective pass-rushing talent (Robert Quinn, Chris Long, etc.), the Rams have been consistently awful. What coaching in the sim league has taught me is that it doesn't so much matter how opposing drives end—only that they do and where. This begs the bigger question: who is more instrumental in ending opposing drives, dominant pass rushers or a dominant secondary?

What does correlate is the relationship between giving up sacks and losing football games. This is another truism that my sim experience has borne out. I gave up a lot of sacks in my 1977 due both to mediocre tackles and to quarterbacks who were sacked a lot in the real 1977 in Brian Sipe and Richard Todd. To wit, the teams that were sacked the most in 2014 were also the worst teams in pro football: Jacksonville surrendered an astonishing seventy-one sacks, Washington was next with fifty-eight, and the Bucs were third with fifty-two. Conversely, New England gave up only twenty-six sacks in 2014, while Peyton Manning and the Broncos gave up only seventeen. This is in part a function of those teams investing in quality linemen but more a function of savvy, veteran quarterbacks. Manning and Brady are among the least athletic quarterbacks in the league in terms of foot speed and quickness, though they are hardly ever sacked. Manning was sacked only 1.06 times per game.

So, collecting a bunch of sacks doesn't necessarily make your team good, but giving up sacks almost certainly makes you bad.

For example, Baltimore's legendary 2000 defense, led by stars like Ray Lewis, Rod Woodson, and Jamie Sharper, collected only thirty-five sacks. That number would have been good enough for only twenty-fourth in the league in 2014. But clearly this was a defense that did other things incredibly well. They allowed only sixteen offensive touchdowns in a sixteen-game season. They limited opponents to only 970 yards rushing—the first team in twenty-two years to keep opponents from gaining 1,000 rushing yards in a season. They led the league in takeaways with forty-nine.

Still, there are examples of good teams getting lots of sacks, but they generally come from bygone eras when pass offenses were less sophisticated and before Bill Walsh introduced the West Coast offense to mitigate against defenses with dominant pass rushes. The great Steeler defenses of 1972–1976 collected 176 sacks over that span and held opponents to only 241 yards per game. Still, though that defensive front was loaded with future Hall of Famers, that averages out to only thirty-five sacks per season. Again, that was a defense that was very good at other things, including getting opponents to turn the football over. Those Steeler defenses amassed a total of 229 takeaways, or an astonishing 45.8 per season. The dominant 1985 Chicago Bears defense took the ball away 3.38 times per game in 1985, which was first in the league. Ditto for the 2013 Seahawks, who took it away 2.4 times per game.

It's not especially novel to note that good teams take the ball away while not themselves giving it away. What interests me is how this relates to player acquisition. Before my 1978 sim season, I fell into the trap of coveting pass rushers. I loved the idea of a defense with a dominant pass rusher or two to create havoc in opposing backfields, so I went for an overpaid Cedric Hardman, who through six games has four sacks. He was dominant in one game for me with three tackles and two sacks but was virtually nonexistent in the others. He is on pace to finish the season with ten or eleven sacks, which is decent, but more importantly, I haven't really seen him as a huge factor in a drive-ending sense.

Let's take a look at a similar player today in Denver's Von Miller. The Broncos made a significant investment in Miller, grabbing him with the second pick of the first round in the 2011 draft. He was selected ahead of receiving standouts A. J. Green and Julio Jones and elite defensive end J. J. Watt. Make no mistake about it, Miller has been sensational. He has forty-nine sacks in fifty-six games. He's been to three Pro Bowls in his short career. However, he has also been shut out, from a sack standpoint, in twenty of those fifty-six games, meaning that over a third of the time he's been on the field, opposing offenses—whether it's game-planning or just a quarterback who knows how to feel the rush and get rid of the ball—have made him irrelevant. And as great as he's been, Watt has been shut out a similar percentage of the time. It's just too easy, in today's offensive climate, to game-plan away from or around the dominant pass rusher. My question is, from a drive-ending standpoint, are we overvaluing these pass rushers? Because what they do is "flashy" and interesting, are we paying too much for what is essentially a situational player?

Now, nobody would argue that Watt is in any way one-dimensional, and even Miller has his moments against the run. But from a value standpoint, how much of an impact on the game does a Von Miller or Cedric Hardman ultimately have?

I should have instead been looking for players who consistently intercept the football or force fumbles. If I'm in the business of purchasing statistics, I should be buying drive-ending turnovers, not an ethereal sack that may or may not actually end a drive and may or may not come at an important point in the game. A sack that happens on second down that is followed by a conversion on third down is basically meaningless. The leading individual sack man on that dominant Baltimore defense? The good-not-great Rob Burnett, with 10.5. Next? Peter Boulware, again a good-not-great player, with 7.5.

The real value on that roster was in the secondary, where each player was a turnover machine. Rod Woodson, a Pro Bowler in 2000, had four interceptions and three fumble recoveries. Strong safety Kim Herring chipped in three picks. Corners Duane Starks and Chris McCallister had six picks and four picks, respectively. They also had an additional three fumble recoveries between them. Starks, McCallister, and Woodson were all first-round selections (Woodson by the Steelers). All told, that secondary accounted for twenty-three

turnovers on their own, which meant that twenty-three opposing drives ended because of the work of the Raven secondary.

The 2002 Tampa Bay Bucs Super Bowl defense was similar in that they generated forty-three sacks, which would have
had them creeping closer to the top of the 2014 list. But the
back end of their defense was similarly turnover-centric, as the
secondary accounted for seventeen drive-ending turnovers.
For what it's worth, the Bucs offense in 2002 was a lot like
Baltimore's 2000 offense in that it won by controlling the
football for long stretches of time and not turning it over.
Quarterback Brad Johnson, while never spectacular, threw
only six interceptions.

The NFL's worst defense in 2014, according to Football
Outsiders' Defensive Drive Stats,[1] were the Atlanta Falcons,
who surrendered 37.7 yards per defensive drive and were on
the field an average of 6.48 plays per drive. Both of these
metrics were worst in the league. They surrendered 2.3 points
per drive, which was thirtieth in the league (Chicago was
worst, giving up 2.52 points per drive). Not surprisingly, the
Falcons were one of the NFL's most disappointing teams, fin-
ishing the season at 6–10 and resulting in the ouster of head
coach Mike Smith. What's interesting is how these drive numbers correlate to things like turnovers and defensive personnel.

The Falcons had a toothless pass rush in 2014, registering
only twenty-two sacks. They gave up thirty-one sacks on the
season, putting them in the middle of the pack with more or
less respectable teams like Dallas and Green Bay. Interestingly, they didn't surrender the football that often either, as they
threw only fifteen interceptions as a team and gave away the
football a total of twenty-three times, placing them in the middle of the pack again. They actually took away the football a

very respectable twenty-eight times, good enough for sixth best in the league. So why weren't the Falcons better? What didn't they do well?

Defensive Drive Data again seems to tell the story. For comparison's sake, let's look at the 2000 Ravens[2] and their dominant defense. As we've discussed before, they were proficient at forcing turnovers and led the league in turnovers per drive (.243) and plays per drive (4.95), which probably has a lot to do with the turnover statistic. They were also the league's best in time of possession per drive (2:14). Not surprisingly, they were best in points per red zone appearance, surrendering an incredibly stingy 2.74 points per opponent's trip. One less sexy statistic is punts per drive. This is another thing that, not surprisingly, the Ravens did well. They were seventh in the league at .460. Good defenses get offenses off the field, often without registering a lot of sacks. And, if the Ravens and 2002 Bucs are any indication, good defenses can win without explosive offenses.

Let's look at drive data on the 2002 Bucs.[3] I bet they were good in the same ways that the flashier 2000 Ravens were good. The Bucs led the league in touchdowns per drive (.093) and plays per drive at 5.07. They were also best in the league at forcing punts per drive at .510. So even when they weren't turning the ball over, they were forcing teams to punt over half the times they had the ball.

A modern defense that has been mentioned in the 1985 Bears/2000 Ravens stratosphere was the 2013 Seahawks. Not surprisingly, their drive data are solid as well. They were first in touchdowns allowed in the red zone, touchdowns per drive (.112), and points in the red zone (3.69) and points per drive.

They also led the league in turnovers per drive with a .201 average.

Let's look at what all of these defenses (2000 Ravens, 2002 Bucs, and 2013 Seahawks) have in common from a personnel standpoint:

1. Their stars are located primarily in the secondary and at defensive tackle. Seattle's big-name, big-money defensive players were located on the back end of its defense in Richard Sherman, Brandon Browner, Earl Thomas, and Kam Chancellor. The Ravens had Woodson at a safety and a pair of first-rounders at corner. The Bucs boasted John Lynch and Ronde Barber in the secondary, with Warren Sapp at defensive tackle.

2. They lack star-type pass rushers. Of these three teams, only Tampa's Simeon Rice could be considered a "star" pass rusher, but even in his case, Tampa was his second career stop, as he was a former first-round (third overall) pick of the Arizona Cardinals. Baltimore's defensive line was the most workman-like in terms of a lack of big names. Seattle got it done with free-agency bargain hits like Cliff Avril and one-dimensional speedsters like Bruce Irvin. The star pass rushers in today's NFL are players like J. J. Watt, Aldon Smith, Von Miller, Cameron Wake, Clay Matthews, Julius Peppers, and Mario Williams. With the exception of Matthews, nobody on that impressive list has a Super Bowl ring.

3. They run a 4-3 scheme.

4. They draft well in later rounds and are shrewd in free agency. Both Barber and Lynch were third-round picks for Tampa, and Baltimore's starting defensive ends on

the 2000 Super Bowl squad were fifth- and seventh-round picks (Rob Burnett and Michael McCrary, respectively) of other teams. But it's the 2013 Seahawks who were true examples of late-round draft greatness, locking up both Sherman and Chancellor in the fifth round along with starting defensive end Red Bryant in the fourth and Brandon Mebane in the third. Super Bowl hero Malcolm Smith was a seventh-round selection.

WEEK SEVEN: DULUTH 31, DETROIT 14: SALVAGE

Detroit's postseason highlight film will be entitled *Great for a Half*, as they took a 14–13 halftime lead into the Silverdome locker room over the Halas Division–leading Duluth Dragons. But the second half belonged to Duluth wide receiver Billy "Alan" Ryckman, who lit up the Silverdome like the Nakatomi Building on Christmas Eve. After repeatedly torching the Lions secondary, he was overheard saying, "YippeKiYay Reggie Rucker." It was that kind of second half for Detroit.

"We went into the game determined to take away Roland Harper, and we dared Joe Ferguson to beat us," said Detroit's embattled coach Kluck. "Unfortunately, Joe Ferguson beat us." Ferguson was overheard saying to coach Randy Sivigny, "Randy, Bubbe, I'm your white knight."

"Like John McClain beating Karl and then wrapping that chain around his neck and leaving him (supposedly) for dead, we didn't finish the job," Kluck explained, never at a loss for *Die Hard* references. "And unlike the movie, in this metaphor he climbed down and then returned to kill all of us. Karl, in this case, being most of the Duluth offense and defense."

"I've been doing this (not the electronic version, paper version)—for 43 years," explains Duluth coach Randy Sivigny, a 47 year old salesman. "I played it back in the days when APBA would make this game in a big box, a card for every guy. I've never met any of these guys (other owners in our league) face-to-face. None of them."

I explain to my son that Sivigny is already one of my favorite owners in the league, as he keeps up a stream of excellent chat banter during the games that serves the twofold purpose of making the game more enjoyable for an owner/coach of a bad team (me) and also serving to humanize my opponent, which keeps me from the kinds of embarrassing opponent-hating outbursts to which I'm prone.

Sivigny, frustrated that he was getting beat by Rucker, my receiver, during our game, chatted, "You know what Rucker rhymes with?" My son shouted with laughter. But the best in-game banter is nostalgic and appreciative.

"I'm really nostalgic," he explains. "I grew up on a farm. We were dirt poor. Sundays we didn't have to work. Watching football for me was everything. I played the APBA game with my brother. He had gotten ahold of all of these old films— Packers in the 1960s and 1970s. Rugged, rough films. I was drawn to all the books. Playing in sim leagues brings back these good feelings for me as a kid.

"Everything in today's football is so quick and fast," he explains. "The media cycle is so fast. I used to read my brother's old *Football Digests*—the articles were really in depth and detailed. They covered the game in depth. There was more of a ground game back then. There were way more interceptions. I'll look that old stuff up on YouTube and watch games.

There's a better flow to the games. I think it's interesting the way the sim league will rank the players versus what the NFL thinks they are.

Sivigny is a die-hard fan and a die-hard gamer. He makes PowerPoints, with videos and pictures, of all of his teams and players. Clearly, he loves football, but he loves it for more than just the feeling that winning provides. He has real affection for the players and the memories that come with them.

"If people really knew it (sim football) existed, a lot more people would play it," he says. "There's almost a social stigma with it where if you're a guy who works hard, you're not supposed to be playing games. The nostalgia part is what gets me and being able to rewrite history. I've turned guys onto this stuff and said 'Here, try this.' And they just go crazy for it.

"This is really competitive. That's the part that I really like about this."

It is no doubt Sivigny's competitiveness that leads him to send me the following e-mail the night after our game. Sivigny, whose team is just a player or two away from seriously contending for a championship, sees my roster as full of the kinds of almost-done-but-still-good players who can push him over the top, and he opened my eyes to the fact that in football, you're either rebuilding or contending. There is no in-between:

> Dear Ted,
>   I have really been examining things and want to get your thoughts. In this game the middle of the road teams can't win. It's like in the NFL in that either you're going for championships or you're rebuilding.

I am going for a championship in the coming years and would be willing to trade away my future (the whole 79 draft and maybe more) for players on your team that are only around for a few years.

Here is my idea and work with me on this. I will send you my whole 1979 1–7 draft for the following players and my reasoning. You won't need the 8–10 picks.

Reggie Rucker 3 year receiver with 43, 52 and 31 catches. All in my wheelhouse

Billy Waddy 3 year receiver with 14, 38, 31 catches. All in my wheelhouse

Dexter Bussey 3 year running back with 144, 145, 105. All in my wheelhouse

Randy Rasmussen guard, one good year left he is an 8/10 next year then goes to a 5 for the last two.

Roger Wehrli, cornerback. He is great, but only for 2 more years, 9/10, 7/10 then 5/10.

I will send you back

Bob Simmons, guard, (good trade player) 6/10, then 5's after that

Ron Bolton, cornerback, bench until 1980, then 8/10 and 6/10

Ken Kennard, defensive tackle, bench until 1981 then 6/10 and 6/10

With my picks you would get at least one 8 year starter, one 5 year starter and a bundle for another 5 year starter. So you give up 5 players for a short term rebuild (3 years) which increases your own pick because you won't be good and get three long term players from me.

Right now you will languish in the 8–12 spot, with this trade you can move up to the 4–7 picks and Hall of Famers for a few years which could set your team up for the future.

Trade Brian Sipe to someone for a high pick, he is only good one year.

I had been trying to "game" the expansion/rebuild system by trying to cobble together a winning roster through a combination of shrewd trading and game-day coaching superiority, which is a great idea except that it isn't working. I need players to win, and, in this league at least, the best players come off the board within the first handful of picks of every draft. My egotistical drive to win right away has created a scenario in which I never really get access to those elite picks because I'm winning my way out of the top of the draft. Randy was kindly trying to tell me to embrace the rebuild. He was also, pragmatically, trying to get me to part with the players who would help him win.

I had a *Moneyball*-esque notion that I could win without elite talent and have won a little but in a macro way have found real, consistent, playoff-type winning to be untenable with my current roster. At some point, it's not just bad breaks, it's a lack of talent. I will need to clean house in the 1979 draft. The reality of this deal is that I've essentially been cultivating players like Bussey and Rucker only to turn around and sell them to another team—turning them into draft picks which I'll use to bring on better, younger players so that, hopefully, I can be a contender myself in a few years.

I pull my son out of bed. "Tris, big trade brewing," I explain over our morning bowls of cereal and then watch as my twelve-year-old dives headlong into the statistical minutiae of a season that happened a full twenty-six years before his birth. "I hate to lose Rucker," he says. I know. I hate it too. I also hate losing Bussey (who was a bedrock of my otherwise-grim 1977 season). Given how hard it is to trade my imaginary sim players, I can only imagine how it feels for real-life general managers. It must be gut wrenching.

The fact of the matter is that punditry is easy and that competition of any kind is hard. It's easy to sit at home, in one's living room, and say, "I could run an NFL team! I can't believe how [Name of General Manager] is screwing it up!" This little sim exercise, on a *much* smaller scale, has given me a whole new appreciation for the almost impossible task laid out for an NFL general manager. It's not easy.

"Let's do the deal," Tristan says, sliding out of the car at school. I wave good-bye to Tris and Maxim for the day and then return home to wave good-bye to Rucker, Bussey, Wehrli, and the rest of my players, who were sim Lions, all for a short period of time. I find myself processing the deal emotionally with Randy.

"Yes, it is very exciting to craft a deal and work with someone," he writes. "No wonder these millionaire owners do this stuff all the time."

EPILOGUE

Week Eight and What I've Learned

My Week Eight 1978 matchup against Buffalo feels, to a certain degree, like the first day of the rest of my sim football life. I traded away the nucleus of my roster—Bussey, Rucker, Rasmussen, and Wehrli—on the hope of future draft choices that will carry me well into the 1980s. The lessons I've learned will hopefully carry me to titles but will also shape the way I watch the "real" game unfolding:

> The Detroit Lions traveled to a blustery Rich Stadium on Sunday afternoon with a far different roster but a renewed sense of hopefulness, having dealt older players for a cache of 1979 draft picks. The result seemed to be a reinvigorated Lions squad, as they led the whole game and won the battle of two very similar 2–5 clubs.
>
> Tight end David Hill was the centerpiece of a retooled offense, catching nine balls for over 150 yards and two scores. Newly acquired wide receiver Luther Blue added eight catches and a touchdown of his own, making his first ball game in a Lions uniform a memorable one. "I'm just

happy to be in Detroit," said Blue following the game. Sipe took advantage of a weak Buffalo secondary in going twenty-eight for forty-five with 316 yards and three touchdowns.

"We continued to feed Kevin Long his carries, both to try to get him going but to also keep the Buffalo defense honest," said head coach Ted Kluck after the game. "But for the first time all year, we let Brian [Sipe] air it out. He took advantage of the matchups he had."

Defensively, the Lions got solid performances from newly acquired cornerback Mike McCoy, a product of the blockbuster trade with Duluth. The Lions also had an interception from defensive end Sherman White and a fumble recovery from Doug Sutherland in the 31–20 victory.

As I move, forward, my core principles are these:

1. In real life, as in sim life, it's less risky and makes more sense to draft an offensive or defensive lineman. These positions "bust" at the lowest rate among first-rounders, making them the safest investment. Oddly, I was blinded by skill-position glory in my 1978 sim draft, choosing Wes Chandler over the solid and long-careered offensive tackle Mike Kenn. I've loved Chandler so far but need to listen to my own advice moving forward.

2. Successful teams run the ball. Given that it's easier to find quality offensive linemen and running backs and given that it's harder to snag an elite, All Pro–caliber franchise quarterback, it makes sense to commit to running the football. The numbers bear this out. Teams that run have better drives, and teams that have more successful drives win the most games. There needs to be

balance, of course, but abandoning the run for a pass-centric offense is folly.

3. It's also foolish to try to draft a franchise quarterback in today's NFL. It just doesn't work. Trade for a quarterback, sign one in free agency, or develop a later-round project. If there's no Peyton Manning or Andrew Luck on the board, don't reach for one. They bust at the highest percentage, so if there's no clear-cut guy there, build an offense that minimizes the position. Teams can still win titles this way.

4. The proliferation of college spread offenses has made it harder for pro teams to buy linemen and quarterbacks right out of college. Shop accordingly.

5. An elite lead-blocking fullback has been a key ingredient in nearly every successful run offense and in the career of nearly every successful running back over the past thirty years. Walter Payton had Matt Suhey. Roger Craig had Tom Rathman. Emmitt Smith had Daryl Johnston. A bunch of guys ran behind Lorenzo Neal and Vonta Leach. Find the next Vonta Leach, and your run game goes to the next level.

6. I want a running back of a certain size, and that size is over 6'0" and 220 pounds.

7. It doesn't necessarily matter where the college pass rusher comes from provided that the pass rusher gets sacks. Height and length also don't matter as much as we think they do provided that the pass rusher brings something else freakish to the table (e.g., Jerome Harrison or Dwight Freeney).

8. Regarding pass rushers, I want football players, not small forwards.

9. That said, having an elite pass rusher doesn't necessarily portend a lot of success in the win/loss column, as sacks probably aren't as important as we (media) make them. The sack is the defense's answer to the glamour statistic and is overblown. Lots of guys have gotten lots of sacks on lots of bad defenses.

10. More important to a defense is turnovers and the ability to stop drives, and, as such, I want cornerbacks who can take away opposing receivers on third down and get interceptions. This is why Darrelle Revis is worth what teams pay him each off-season.

11. The draft is overblown. It's just another way to acquire players and fill out a fifty-three-man roster. If you can use draft picks as currency to purchase the player you want—do that, as the Jets did this off-season stealing Brandon Marshall from Chicago with a fifth-round pick.

I have also had an incredible amount of fun with the new friends I've met in the Odyssey Football League, many of whom are old enough to be my father. Their banter has been lively, gracious, and saturated with a knowledge of football history. I have learned that to a large degree, much of the joy of competition is simply in participating—in being in the fray. I have learned a whole new level of respect not only for the men who play the games but also for the men who make personnel decisions at a high level. Their jobs are extremely complicated and are made further complicated by the fact that they are real men in real relationships with real players who all have needs, families, and backstories.

I have learned that it is important to keep a human face on what can, even as I write about statistical analysis, be a dehu-

manizing entertainment product. From the helmets that ob-
scure their faces and the numbers that adorn their uniforms,
it's easy to think of players simply as human commodities. In
an odd way, I've had as much fun seeking out the personal
player stories of 1978 as I have had analyzing their statistics.

I've learned that football is for fathers and sons. For me,
this meant lifting weights, running, and throwing the ball with
my own father, who drove me all over the Midwest to see all
manner of live football games from Blackford High School to
Ball State to Indiana to the Indianapolis Colts. It meant his
being there for all of the highs and lows of my career—from
the recruiting visit to Indiana to the evening I told him in his
bedroom that I was done playing college football. His grace
was a lesson to me.

I've learned that it's more important to be with my son, in
football, than it is to see him perform well. He loves the game,
but I don't think he loves it as much as I do, and for that I'm
glad. The game transcended joyful competition for me and
became combat. The times I've spent coaching these sim
games with him and seeing his gifted analytical mind whirl
have brought me joy.

ACKNOWLEDGMENTS

I'd like to thank Brandon Rose, commissioner of the Odyssey Football League (OFL), for returning my e-mails and letting me join what is a roving fraternity of classy and knowledgeable football fans. It is Brandon's hours of computer work each week that keep the league—and the good times—rolling. I've looked forward with as much interest to his casual e-mails about Alabama football, Kenny Stabler, and his son, who is himself a promising young sports journalist. Special thanks as well to the rest of the members of the OFL, especially Randy Sivigny and Edward "Abe" Brown, whose insights and lively trade banter have been invaluable.

Thanks to Mike Urban of Lyons Press for taking on a slightly strange and nostalgic sports project and to my literary agent Andrew Wolgemuth for guiding my career in the same way that John Madden captained the Oakland Raider misfits under his watch in the 1970s. Andrew, you have a tough job, and I appreciate what you do.

Thanks to my lovely wife Kristin for putting up with the buying and archiving of retro football books, videos, and other random memorabilia. You are a saint.

To Tristan Kluck, my son and steadfast, trusted assistant coach. I love you buddy. Coaching with you is a joy. I've learned a lot from you this season!

And to Ted Kluck. My father, my role model, and an original 1970s headbanger. Thank you for teaching me how to work and how to love the game.

All statistical data are from www.pro-football-reference.com.

NOTES

2. RUNNING ON EMPTY

1. www.footballoutsiders.com/stat-analysis/2006/college-quarterbacks-through-prism-statistics.

3. EVERY WHICH WAY
BUT LOOSE

1. Examples from 2014 alone include Jim Harbaugh and his general manager; Robert Griffin III and his coach, Jay Gruden; and Jay Cutler.

2. Paul Zimmerman, "What's Wrong with the NFL?," *Sports Illustrated*, November 12, 1984, 30–31.

5. A LONG HANDOFF

1. NFL.com/combine/profiles/Adrian-Hubbard?id=2543686.

7. IN PRAISE OF THE
GENTLEMAN FAN

1. D. T. Max, *Every Love Story Is a Ghost Story: A Life of David Foster Wallace* (New York: Penguin, 2012), 156.

2. Max, *Every Love Story Is a Ghost Story*, 156.

3. Max, *Every Love Story Is a Ghost Story*, 186.

4. "Cocaine and a Super Bowl Team: The Last Straw: Drugs in the NFL: A Chronology," *Los Angeles Times*, January 29, 1986.

5. Armen Keteyian, *Big Red Confidential: Inside Nebraska Football* (New York: Contemporary Books, 1989).

6. "Earl Campbell: Addiction to Painkillers and His Campaign to Help Others," *Yahoo! Sports: The Postgame*, October 29, 2013.

7. "Hall of Famer Earl Campbell to Have Nerve Treatment, Says It 'ame from Playing the Way I Did,'" FoxNews.com, September 18, 2012.

8. Joe Henderson, "Ex-Bucs Running Back's Mind Strays Wildly, a Likely Consequence of Multiple Concussions," *Tampa Tribune*, July 25, 2010.

8. IT'S AN ANSWER

1. This was initially written in 2013. Bush is no longer there.

2. Incidentally, Vereen's full name is Shane Patrick-Henry Vereen, meaning that his parents must have had a special affinity for the eighteenth-century orator and leader of the Virginia independence movement.

9. THE JOY OF SACKS, PART I

1. Armen Keteyian, *Big Red Confidential: Inside Nebraska Football* (New York: Contemporary Books, 1989), 228.

11. SCOUTING PARADIGMS

1. Jack Bechta, "Are NFL Scouting Department Under-funded?," National Football Post, www.nationalfootballpost.com/Are-NFL-scouting-departments-underfunded, April 12, 2011.

2. Robert Seidman, "NFL Draft on ESPN Reaches Record Total Audience of 36.7 Million Viewers," TV by the Numbers, tvbythenumbers.zap2it.com/2009/04/28/nfl-draft-on-espn-reaches-record-total-audience-of-367-million-viewers/17588, April 28, 2009.

12. THE JOY OF SACKS, PART II

1. www.footballoutsiders.com/stats/drivestatsdef2014.
2. www.footballoutsiders.com/stats/drivestatsdef2000.
3. www.footballoutsiders.com/stats/drivestatsdef2002.

INDEX

ABOUT THE AUTHOR

Ted Kluck is the award-winning author of more than a dozen books. Ted's work has appeared in *ESPN the Magazine*, *Sports Spectrum Magazine*, and ESPN.com Page 2. A bimonthly column for *Sports Spectrum Magazine* titled "Pro and Con" won the Evangelical Press Association award for best standing column in 2003. Ted is the author of *Robert Griffin III: Athlete, Leader, Believer* (2013) and collaborator for NFL Hall of Famer Jim Kelly on *Playbook for Dads* (2012).

Ted played a season of professional indoor football with the Battle Creek (Michigan) Crunch of the Continental Indoor Football League and lived to tell about it in *Paper Tiger: One Athlete's Journey to the Underbelly of Pro Football* (2007). Part homage to George Plimpton and part gritty travelogue through the dingy arenas and bus trips that make up minor league football, this book was named a Michigan Notable Book for 2008, joining the ranks of such authors as Jim Harrison and Elmore Leonard.

Game Time: Inside College Football (2007) is a collection of scene pieces and interviews that Ted put together from all levels of college football. Included are features on a coach who tried to integrate the football program at Jackson State, a walk-on at the University of Michigan, a Heisman Trophy winner committed to rebuilding the inner city of New Orleans, and the annual NFL meat market that is the Senior Bowl in Mobile, Alabama.

Ted's first book, *Facing Tyson: Fifteen Fighters, Fifteen Stories*, features interviews with fifteen men who fought Mike Tyson. Ted met these men in their homes, their gyms, and their streets, providing a fascinating look at this savage sport and the men who populate it.

Ted has played professional indoor football, coached high school football, trained as a professional wrestler, served as a missionary, and taught writing courses at the college level. He lives in Grand Ledge, Michigan, with his wife Kristin and sons Tristan and Maxim, where he writes, teaches, and speaks.